THE PSYCHOLOGY OF BLACKS: AN AFRO-AMERICAN PERSPECTIVE

JOSEPH L. WHITE
University of California—Irvine

Prentice-Hall, Inc., Englewood Cliffs, New Jersey 07632

Library of Congress Cataloging in Publication Data

White. Joseph L., 1932-
  The psychology of Blacks : an Afro-American perspective.

  Includes bibliographies and index.
  1. Afro-Americans—Psychology. I. Title.
E185.625.W47   1984   305.8'96073   83-11203
ISBN 0-13-735134-8

© 1984 by Prentice-Hall, Inc., Englewood Cliffs, New Jersey 07632

Printed in the United States of America

10 9 8 7 6 5 4 3 2 1

Editorial/production supervision: Virginia Cavanagh Neri
Cover design: Jeanette Jacobs
Manufacturing buyer: Ron Chapman

ISBN 0-13-735134-8

Prentice-Hall International, Inc., *London*
Prentice-Hall of Australia Pty. Limited, *Sydney*
Editora Prentice-Hall do Brasil, Ltda., *Rio de Janeiro*
Prentice-Hall Canada Inc., *Toronto*
Prentice-Hall of India Private Limited, *New Delhi*
Prentice-Hall of Japan, Inc., *Tokyo*
Prentice-Hall of Southeast Asia Pte. Ltd., *Singapore*
Whitehall Books Limited, *Wellington, New Zealand*

To the memory of Dorothy Lee White, who left a model of human vitality, humor, resourcefulness, and strength in the face of adversity for her children, Bunkey, Mary Jane, and Joe to use as guidelines for living.

COLORED TOWN

Where the sun is always burnin' and it gets so hot
and there's drunk musicians playin' at the streetcar stop
and the bar-b-que you're smellin' is the best around.
You can bet that you're in colored town.

When the day begins at five with a scrubbin' pail and rag
and she hides her workin' clothes in a Penny's shoppin' bag
and the old man tips his hat and says "good-day, Miz Brown."
You can bet that you're in the black man's town.

"Ladonna change the baby cause I think she's wet;
can you watch the kids, I got to get the welfare check;
chi'l I done tol' you, keep that t.v. down."
You can bet that you're in the poor man's town.

When you go to church on Sunday in your finest things
and you say "amen" and "yes Lawd" when the choir sings
and you fix up greens and cornbread, have the preacher round.
You can bet that you're in the Lord's own town.

"Girl; let me tell you 'bout the fight I had with my man,
I went upside his head with a fryin' pan,
do you know I knocked him out, he didn't make a sound."
You can bet that you're in the sisters' town.

Where they press hair at the corner, barber shop next door
and you dance till five on Friday till your feet get sore
and you hear Aretha singin' for ten blocks around.
You can bet that you're in the soul man's town.

When your best friend throws a party just to pay his rent
and he charges all the neighbors about "fifty cent"
and the cops come by to tell you, "turn the music down."
You can bet that you're in the brothers' town.

Now life down on the east side ain't all fun and games:
there was the time November last year, they shot brother James
and they held his mama when they put him in the ground.
You can bet that you're in a different town.

You can't cry about tomorrow, you do what you can
and you hope that someday you will see the Promised Land
so before you go to sleep your knees hit the ground.
You can bet that you're in colored town.

Lori Suzanne White
Granddaughter of Dorothy Lee White

CONTENTS

FOREWORD

We witnessed a renewed interest in the psychology of Afro-Americans in the late 1960s and 1970s. To be certain there has been a steady stream of books and articles on the psychological dimensions of Afro-American behavior for well over 100 years. But during the period of the Great Society there was renewed and intensified study of Afro-Americans, and with it a revival and extension of deficiency based and pejorative explanations of black behavior. The writings of the 1970s and 1980s—unlike the work of the several immediately preceding decades—involved black social scientists as active and significant contributors to the literature, who in comprehensive volumes wrote persuasively on the psychological dimensions of black behavior in contemporary (Williams, *Black Psychology: Compelling Issues and Views*, 1978; Jones, *Black Psychology* 1972, 1980; Jenkins, *The Psychology of the Afro-American: A Humanistic Approach*, 1982) and historical (Guthrie, *Even the Rat Was White: A Historical View of Psychology*, 1976) perspectives. We also witnessed scores of articles written by black social scientists, and an increasing number of theses and dissertations written by black graduate students who presented compelling alternative viewpoints on the extant Eurocentrically oriented explanations of black behavior.

But even in the 1960s and later, black scholars—by their own report—continued to be plagued by inaccessibility to mainstream journals for presentation of their research, theories, and explanations which, in their view, challenged the conventional wisdom. It is not surprising, therefore, that Professor Joseph White's seminal 1970 article, "Toward A Black Psychology," which emphasized that traditional theories simply did not have sufficient explanatory power to account for the behavior of black people, first appeared in *Ebony*, a general circulation black magazine, and that its earlier version appeared in the *Black Scholar*, a journal devoted to general issues in the social sciences and humanities whose major readership is black intellectuals. These are important audiences, to be sure, but not the only ones for the important message of White's article, which should have received the attention of all members of the professional social science community who create and market theories of black behavior for policymakers and the general scientific community. It is entirely fitting, then, that Professor White, whose seminal papers captured the need for a psychology of Afro-Americans, and who has chronicled important developments in this field, now takes upon himself the task of presenting an integrated and conceptually coherent psychological portrait of Afro-Americans. As the reader will soon discover, White has carried out this assignment with remarkable skill.

Chapter One lays the framework for the book and appropriately draws upon diverse disciplines to document the uniqueness of Afro-American experiences that support the need for a "Psychology of Blacks." The utility of the framework is then convincingly demonstrated through its application to such areas as the black family (Chapter Three), child development (Chapter Four), educational psychology (Chapter Five), and mental

health (Chapter Six). In an exciting chapter on black language, oral literature, and expressive patterns (Chapter Two), White identifies psychological
themes unique to the black experience, a creative analysis indeed. And in
this chapter, as in others, White draws upon a variety of humanities and
social science disciplines to adduce the patterns he describes.

The reader will find that Professor White's lanuage is at once colorful
and precise, and that it richly captures the flavor of the subject matter; the
reading is engrossing. The reader will also find that Professor White has
produced a work which defines an agenda for research which is likely to
engage scholars of the Afro-American experience for some time. That is to
say, Professor White has advanced a series of intuitively appealing hypotheses and propositions which are highly representative, I feel, of the psychological reality of black people and which will surey be the grist for further
research and study.

White's book is a significant addition to the scholarship in Afro-
American Psychology and represents an important resource for those desir-
ing a comprehensive and conceptually coherent overview of work in this
area, as well as a stimulus for those who wish to undertake research on the
provocative propositions he advances.

Reginald L. Jones

PREFACE

This book is about the psychological perspective which is reflected in the behavior, attitudes, life styles, and cultural heritage of Black Americans.

From Afro-American folklore, literature, direct observations, and the writings of Black psychologists, I have identified the primary dimensions in the psychological space of Afro-Americans. These dimensions openness to self and others, tragedy and resilience, psychological connectedness and interdependence, the oral tradition, creative synthesis, fluid time perception, the value of direct experience, and respect for the elderly, constitute a definitive Black ethos which Afro-Americans use as a frame of reference to interpret the world around them, establish guidelines for living and are expressed in family dynamics, child rearing, teaching, and learning and actualization patterns.

At the root of the Black psychological perspective is a distinctive African cultural influence which has persisted despite the fact that Black Americans have lived in the United States for over 350 years. The persistence of the African influence on the psyche of Black Americans is discussed within the context of a rationale that traces the continuity of Afro-American psychological styles across time and space.

The psychological model presented herein concentrates on the strengths of Afro-Americans and can be contrasted to the deficit-deficiency model of Black psychology which has been advanced by Euro-American psychologists.

This book was written to facilitate an understanding of Black psychological dynamics on the part of behavioral sciences, human service workers, educators, policy makers, and members of the nonprofessional public who have an interest in learning more about the psychological perspective of Black Americans. It can also be utilized as a primary or supplementary text for college level courses in Black psychology or cross-cultural psychology.

I would like to express my appreciation to those who read the manuscript and offered comments: Carolyn Murray, University of California, Riverside; and Pearl Dansby, Tennessee State University.

Joseph L. White

CHAPTER ONE

BASIC ASSUMPTIONS AND HISTORICAL BACKDROP

INTRODUCTION

This book will be organized around the premise that there is a distinctive, coherent, persistent Afro-American psychological perspective, frame of reference, world view, or cultural ethos that is evident in the behavior, attitudes, feelings, life styles, and expressive patterns of Black Americans. A psychological perspective, frame of reference, world view, or cultural ethos is a set of assumptions, beliefs, values, ideas, and behaviors shared by a particular group of people that are transmitted from one generation to the next. This composite set of values, ideas, and beliefs provides people with a way of interpreting reality and relating to others and a general design for living. The cultural ethos or world view functions like a set of glasses that focuses reality, filters impressions, and gives meaning to events (Nobles, 1977).

The Afro-American psychological perspective, the foundation for the psychology of Blackness, is characterized by seven interrelated primary dimensions: openness to self and others, tragedy and resilience, psychological connectedness and interdependence, the oral tradition, creative synthesis, fluid time perception, and the value of direct experience combined with respect for the elderly. The psychology of Blackness is reflected in the family, close relationships, child rearing, language, learning styles, and patterns of psychological actualization, and it tends to become more visible when the public and private behavior of Black folks is observed in a wide variety of situations over an extended period of time. The primary themes of the Afro-American frame of reference are expressed in Black oral literature, song, dance, and history; they appear as major issues in the works of Black authors Langston Hughes (1934, 1961, 1965), Richard Wright (1964, 1966), Ralph Ellison (1947, 1964), and James Baldwin (1955, 1963, 1965) and are set forth as basic assumptions in the writings of contemporary Black psychologists Charles Thomas (1970, 1971), Robert Williams (1974, 1975), Wade Nobles (1972, 1976), William Cross (1971, 1980), and Robert Guthrie (1976, 1980).

At the root of the Afro-American frame of reference is an identifiable African cultural influence that has persisted despite the continuing exposure of the Black American psyche to the Euro-American culture during the past 350 and more years of geographical and temporal separation from Africa. Black psychology, the psychology of blackness, is the attempt to build a conceptual model to organize, explain, and understand the psychosocial behavior of Black Americans based on the primary dimensions of an Afro-American world view.

THE AFRO-AMERICAN WORLD VIEW

A quality of spontaneity, openness to feelings, and emotional vitality is expressed in the behavior styles of Black folks. People are expected to be for real, down-to-earth, authentic, genuine (Staples, 1976), and willing to take the risk of sharing, as opposed to repressing, the range of human feelings expressed in the joy and sadness of Black gospel music and the sensualness and hardship of the blues. In the Black experience tragedy is unavoidable. Resilience and revitalization of the human spirit are facilitated by the use of humor and by the knowledge that one is not alone, there are others who will bear witness to the profound sorrows of existence. Through this sharing, beginning with the extended family, we reach out and touch others and are connected to them in a series of interdependent relationship networks guided by a spirit of cooperation and mutual aid, beginning with the extended family. These interdependent relationships and social networks are connected across time and space by the oral tradition, the power of the spoken word. The spoken word, the language of Afro-Americans, represents a shared participatory space in which both speaker and listener continuously affirm each other's presence within the context of a call–response dialogue. The goal in Black social interaction and language patterns is to be able to move harmoniously with the rhythm of what's happening, to be in time and in touch with the flow, pace, and tempo of events as opposed to being on time. Time is not a commodity rigidly controlled by a metric system, but a series of events that are experienced and shared with others throughout the course of the life cycle (Smitherman, 1977). The emphasis in the Black experience is on being together, coming together, and getting it together with a focus on the commonalities of a collective experience, as opposed to the diversities. This creative synthesis and harmonious blending can be seen at political rallies in the Black community when the audience tends to cheer, cosign, and amen speakers with widely divergent points of view. According to the late Malcolm X (1966), the audience intuitively knows that the speakers, whatever their point of view or political affiliation, are all trying to deal with the common themes of freedom, liberation, and getting "the man" off Black people's backs.

The elderly in the Black community are valued because they are the storehouse of the oral tradition, the basic teachings of life. They have experienced life, have been through the repetitive cycle of birth, death, joy, sorrow, and revitalization, and have survived. They have their life more together than the young folks who have not paid any dues and may not even know there are dues to be paid.

At the core of the Afro-American world view with its emphasis on human vitality, openness to feelings, collective sharing, mutual support, and creative synthesis is a holistic, humanistic conception of human beings and how they should relate to each other (Jeffers, 1971).

THE AFRICAN WORLD VIEW

The holistic, humanistic philosophy is the principle feature in the African ethos described by Nobles (1972) and Mbiti (1970). There appears to be a definite correspondence between the African ethos and the Afro-American world view in terms of the focus on emotional vitality, interdependence, collective survival, the oral tradition, perception of time, harmonious blending, and the role of the elderly.

The African world view begins with a holistic conception of the human condition. There is no mind–body or affective–cognitive dualism. The human organism is conceived as a totality made up of a series of interlocking systems. This total person is simultaneously a feeling, experiencing, sensualizing, sensing, and knowing human being living in a dynamic, vitalistic world where everything is interrelated and endowed with the supreme force of life. There is a sense of aliveness, intensity, and animation in the music, dance, song, language, and life styles of Africans. Emotions are not labeled as bad; therefore, there is no need to repress feelings of compassion, love, joy, or sensuality.

The basic human unit is the tribe, not the individual. The tribe operates under a set of rules geared toward collective survival. Cooperation is therefore valued above competition and individualism. The concept of alienation is nonexistent in African philosophy since the people are closely interconnected with each other in a way of life that involves concern and responsibility toward others. In a framework that values collective survival, where people are psychologically interdependent on each other, active aggression against another person is in reality an act of aggression against oneself (Nobles, 1976). The idea of interrelatedness extends to the whole universe, arranged in a hierarchy that includes God, humans, animals, plants, and inanimate objects in a descending order.

People are linked together in a geographical and temporal frame by the oral tradition, with messages being transmitted across time and space by word of mouth or the drums. Each tribe contains a *griot,* an oral historian, who is a living record of the people's heritage. The spoken word is revered. Words take on a quality of life when they are uttered by the speaker. In the act of *Nommo* the speaker literally breathes life into a word. Nothing exists, including newborn babies, until a name has been uttered with the breath of life. When words are spoken, the listener is expected to acknowledge receiving the message by responding to the speaker. This is known as the call–response. The speaker sends out a message or a call, and the listener makes a response indicating that he or she has heard the message. The speaker and the listener operate within a shared psycholinguistic space affirming each other's presence.

Time is marked off by a series of events that have been shared with others in the past or are occurring in the present. Thus, when an African talks about time in the past tense, reference points are likely to be established by events such as a daughter's marriage or a son's birth, events that were shared with others. When an African is trying to make arrangements about meeting someone in the immediate future, a specific time, such as three o'clock, is avoided. The person is more likely to say, "I will meet you after I finish milking the cows." The primary time frames in African languages are past and present. There is no word in most African languages for the distant future. The distant future has not yet happened; therefore, it does not exist. In this fluid perception of time there is no guilt about wasting time. Time is not a monetary commodity but an experience to be shared with others.

Time is also considered to be repetitive. The major events used to designate points in time, such as conception, birth, the naming ceremony, puberty, and marriage, repeat themselves throughout the life cycle. There is a cyclical, rhythmic pattern to the flow of events—the coming and going of the seasons, the rising and the setting of the sun, and the movement through the stages of life. Nature's rhythms are believed to have been put in order by God, who knew what He was doing. The essence of life is to be able to move harmoniously with the cyclical rhythms of the universe's internal clock. The goal is not to control or dominate the universe, but to blend creatively into the tempo and pace of the seasons of life. Life is broken down into a series of stages beginning with conception, followed by birth, the naming ceremony, puberty, initiation rites, marriage, adulthood, and old age. Death is seen as a stage of life. The living dead are still members of the tribe, and personal immortality is assured as long as one's memory is continuously passed down to each generation by the tribe's oral historian. Since immortality is guaranteed by the passing of one's memory forward, there is no pervasive fear of old age and death. The tribal elders are valued because they have accumulated the wisdoms of life's teachings. In the hierarchical arrangement of the cosmos they occupy a position just below that of the Supreme Being and the living dead.

THE PERSISTENCE
OF THE AFRICAN WORLD VIEW

The African influence persisted in Black life in America because it provided a familiar pattern of customs, folklore, and beliefs about the supernatural and collective survival, allowing the early Afro-Americans to establish a sense of meaning and direction in the world around them. By holding onto the roots of the African ethos, the slaves and their descendants were able to create a collective psychological space, independent of the oppressor, where they could generate a sense of worth, dignity, and belonging (Gutman, 1976; Fredrickson, 1976).

This collectively shared psychological space served as a protective screen that prevented the slaves from internalizing the oppressor's view of white superiority and Black inferiority. Within this shared psychological space, Blacks have been able to attach completely different cultural meanings to the white man's concepts of bad and good. For example, in Afro-American folklore, "bad niggers"—angry, defiant, fearless niggers who are considered to be extremely undesirable by the white man are held in awe and admiration.

The remnants of the African tradition within Black culture were handed down from generation to generation by the oral tradition operating within informal and formal communal institutions such as the Black church, extended family networks, fraternal orders, women's clubs, and street corner society. The continuing presence of the African tradition in contemporary Afro-America is exemplified in the Black church. The content is Euro-American, but the style and form shows a definite African influence (Nobles, 1977). In the "git'-down" Black Baptist church where the soul folks righteously take care of business every Sunday morning (and sometimes all afternoon), the content of the service is Euro-American. Black people pray from a Bible written in English, the language of the songs and sermons are in English, or at least what some people might refer to as an Afro-American version of English, but the similarity ends here. Anyone who has observed the joy, spontaneity, call–response language between preacher and congregation, the amen corner, and the close fellowship of the flock has been provided with a visual-auditory demonstration of the continuing presence of an African influence.

Traditional scholars have been unwilling to recognize the presence of an African influence in Black life styles. According to this view, whatever existed in the way of African culture was stamped out by the brutal effects of slavery and the subsequent economic, legal, and political oppression. Afro-Americans are solely the product of American society (Elkins, 1959). To the extent that differences between Euro-Americans and Afro-Americans exist, they represent inferior approximations on the part of Black Americans, attempts to imitate Euro-Americans rather than intrinsically different cultural and psychosocial styles. This type of thinking is at the core of the pathology, deficit, deprivation models of Black inferiority. The revisionists (Blassingame, 1972; Gutman, 1976; Rawick, 1972; and Nobles, 1974) who have emerged in recent years take the view that the slaves had cultural and psychological resources of their own, from which emerged the range and complexity of Afro-American life styles we see today. They reject the view that the slaves were only empty vessels who were acted upon, shaped, and dominated by Euro-American society. They do not reject the influence of Euro-American values on Afro-Americans. They view blackness or Black culture as representing an admixture of two world views coming together, with the African world view as its guiding foundation (Nobles, 1974).

The presence of Afro-American values is not always apparent in the public behavior of brothers and sisters. Some Blacks, typified by Nathan Hare's *Black Anglo Saxon* (1965) and E. Franklin Frazier's *Black Bourgeoisie* (1962), attempt to deny all traces of Afro-American life styles in their behavior. They consider Euro-American cultural values and expressive styles to be superior. In commenting on how the Black race had prospered under the guidance of white folks, Booker T. Washington (1932), one of the leading Black spokespersons at the turn of the century, was reported to have said that Black folks went into slavery as pagans and came out as Christians, went into slavery without language and came out speaking the beautiful Anglo-Saxon tongue. In less guarded moments, however, many of these Black Anglo-Saxons show evidence of having internalized definite aspects of the Black culture. Nathan Hare (1965) describes a group of Black classical music majors who were listening to and discussing the finer nuances of the music of Euro-American composers when unbeknownst to them someone put on a blues-and-rhythm tune by a popular Black singer. Despite their denials of having ever heard of this Black performer, the brothers and sisters were soon popping their fingers and dancing in time with the music. Hare's anecdote suggests that all Black Americans have internalized in varying degrees the behaviors, attitudes, and expressive patterns of the Afro-American ethos. Many of us are aware of the brothers who in their daily speech try to affect totally the tone, pace, and diction of standard oral English, yet their whole language demeanor changes when they fall into the "mama you sho' is fine" love rapping designed to get them over with some super fine sister.

During the heightened Black consciousness of the late 1960s and early 1970s, many of the Black bourgeoisie went through a identity transformation, reflected by a change in the level of their awareness, from Negro to Black. The stages in this identity transformation are described by Thomas (1971) and Cross (1971). In the first stage, called the preencounter or Negromacy stage, the person has a very negative impression of blackness, sees Euro-American culture as much more sophisticated, and is likely to criticize Black folks for not working hard enough, talking too loud, and spending too much time "boogalooing." In the second stage, the encounter stage, the Nego has encountered a major personal disappointment in his or her attempts to aspire to Euro-American expectations. He or she discovers that structural oppression in the United States is real, and that white folks do not mean what they say about fair play and justice for all. Concomitantly comes the discovery that there is some substance to Afro-Americans and the cultural heritage that has enabled them to survive and keep on climbin', despite the fact that they have been denied and continue to be denied the full range of opportunity in American life. This is followed by the immersion stage. In the immersion stage the person becomes obsessed with blackness, Afro-American culture, and the African heritage. His or her appearance becomes distinctly Afro, probably with an overgrown bush augmented by a colorful daishiki, and his or her rhetoric takes on a tone of super blackness. In interactions with other Blacks at meetings and gatherings, those in the immersion stage find it necessary to demonstrate frequently how Black they are by giving long, rambling testimony bearing self-witness to how together they are now, how many dues they have paid, how evil white folks are, and how they have been Black longer than anybody else. They might even describe their early identity as Black Anglo-Saxons as a massive deception, a game they were running on "the man" as undercover Uncle Toms. In the final stage of Black awareness, the universal stage, the person completes the Negro to Black transformation. Blacks who have reached this stage feel more secure, have internalized the Afro-American ethos into their life space, don't need to announce their blackness endlessly, understand that everybody doesn't have to share their exact belief system in order to be relevant, and can identify with the liberation struggles of other oppressed peoples.

At the other end of the Black identity continuum, the remnants of African culture are highly visible in the behavioral patterns and languages of the "Geeches" who live on the sea islands off the coast of Georgia. These Blacks whose ancestors were brought here direct from West Africa have been culturally isolated from the main stream of both Black and white America for decades. The sounds and syntax patterns in their speech as well as the nearly six hundred words used in personal names, nicknames, song, and dances are almost identical to those used in Ibo, Yoruba, Mandingo, and Wolof languages of West Africa (Smitherman, 1977).

One can think of Black Americans as being spread along a cultural spectrum, the majority representing a combination of both African and American culture (blackness) somewhere between the Geeches who show almost pure Africanism in their behavior at one extreme and the Black Anglo-Saxons who attempt to deny any traces of the African ethos at the other.

THE EURO-AMERICAN WORLD VIEW

The Afro-American and African world views can be differentiated from the Euro-American world view. At the heart of the Euro-American world view is the problem of the mind–body dualism inherited from Descrates. This dualistic thinking has generated a number of dichotomies along the lines of rational–irrational, ego–id, good–bad, affective–cognitive, human–animal, primitive–civilized, and master–slave. These dichotomies in turn have led to questions of inferiority–superiority, better–worse, and debate as to which side of the dualism should control human behavior. In the Protestant ethic the feeling processes were considered the bad, destructive element in the human condition, an element that needed to be controlled by the mind. Feelings were sinful, evil, destructive, animalistic, and a reflection of the evil that must be resolved before humans could achieve salvation and develop an advanced civilization with its attendant discontents. It was necessary to create the unconscious mind to be the storehouse of the bad instincts, sensual drives, and aggressive urges within the human organism, and to have these bad instincts controlled by the good forces represented by the ego and superego (Freud, 1923, 1930). Aggression during wars, however, was sanctioned because the wars were rationally justified under the sacred banners of God, justice, and country. Sexual exploitation of captive women was also permitted as the spoils of war, but I am not sure this was justified by God.

The basic human unit in the Euro-American world view is the individual, who is considered as separate, distinct, alone, apart from and independent of others. In the context of the Euro-American philosophy of limits, there is only so much room at the top of the pyramid, which means there must be winners and losers, survivors and nonsurvivors. The key to winning and surviving is rugged individualism, competition, and establishing power, dominance, and control by manipulating others (Shostrom, 1967).

The language tradition of Euro-Americans is visual-written. Records of events, history, narratives, contracts, and rules are transmitted by means of the written word. Previous generations of anthropologists considered the presence of a written language as evidence of the Anglo-Saxon's advanced civilization, despite a history of written promises that were not kept where people of color were concerned. In situations where the spoken word is being used, the speaker and the listener maintain a separate psychological space. Speech is delivered in a controlled, low-keyed, detached, and slow-paced tempo. The listener is expected to wait until the speaker finishes the message before a reply is given. Any animated cries of "right on," "speak" and "yes, Lord" from the listener during the speaker's delivery would be considered out of order in proper Euro-American language circles.

Time is a precisely measured commodity in a linear system that clearly designates the time frames of present, past, and future. By the same token, the language system has precise conjugations of the verb *to be* to indicate whether an event is happening now, has happened in the past or will happen in the future. Euro-Americans do not say "he be walkin'," they say "he is walking now," "he was walking yesterday," "he will be walking tomorrow," or "he is always walking." Time is not considered to be repetitive. Once the moment is experienced, it is gone forever, you cannot go home again, and no man ever steps in the same river twice.

Time is oriented toward work, future, and money. If time is properly invested in hard work over an extended period of time, there should be a future payoff in money, status, achievement, or a higher position in heaven. An idle mind is the devil's workshop, time is not to be wasted, and a guilty conscience is the consequence of wasted time. This is the old Protestant work ethic that generations of Euro-American children have been taught. In the work ethic, feelings, spontaneity, fun, and sensuality are considered to be highly undesirable. Since there is only a limited amount of time and human energy, investments of time and energy in emotionally satisfying experiences can only detract from efforts toward future gains through hard work. Therefore, the way to economic and social advancement was to suppress potentially gratifying activities and invest the accumulated human energy in work and work-related efforts. The Euro-American views about work, economic gain, and psychological growth come together in the economic and psychological theories of Sigmund Freud (1930) and Adam Smith (1880); save up the libido, redirect the accumulated energies into socially approved channels, and grow rich psychologically, which is analogous to saving your money, reinvesting the interest in additional savings, and growing rich economically.

The concept of manifest destiny has been very prominent in the thinking, behavior, and cultural attitudes of Euro-Americans. Anglo-Saxons, northern Europeans, the Nordic stocks, and their American descendants have marched across the globe operating under the belief that they were ordered by God Himself to take over the universe; first the earth, then the moon, the stars, and even life itself through the manipulation of genetic codes. Their interactions with other peoples have been governed by power, dominance, and control. An attitude of cultural superiority has persisted to the present day. Differences between people, whether by race, geography, life style, or even sex were not seen as opportunities for mutual enrichment through creative synthesis, but as an opportunity to take over, oppress, and impose their leadership on other people (Comer, 1969).

Death has been a very difficult issue for the Euro-American culture to deal with. Despite the power and control of modern science with its life support systems and organ transplants, the human organism passes through a life cycle that ends in death. The presence of death is evidence of the Euro-American's mortality and lack of omnipotence. Ideas about immortality and heaven with Jesus may be temporarily soothing, but very few Euro-Americans voluntarily want to leave life on this earth to be with sweet Jesus in heaven. Death is denied and feared (Aries, 1980); its occurrence is not commemorated as a celebration of life. Euro-Americans are obsessed with the idea of eternal youth. The accent on youth represents an attempt to deny the process of aging, which brings us closer to death. The elderly are definitely not valued. Like death itself, there is an attempt to deny the existence of the elderly by placing them in nursing homes far from the center of the family's daily activities. It is a tragedy that many young children in America have been prevented from developing the kind of day-to-day relationship with the elderly that would allow them to share the wisdom these senior citizens have built up through a lifetime.

EURO-AMERICAN PSYCHOLOGY
AND THE CONCEPT OF BLACKNESS

The Euro-American world view spawned a reductionistic psychology concerned with categorization, mental measurement, and the establishment of norms. The primary unit of study was the individual, and emphasis was centered on the early years of child development. Differences and diversity from established norms were treated as deviant. Unacceptable thoughts, feelings, and impulses were regulated into the unconscious. Despite claims of scientific objectivity in the measurement of mental abilities, the outcome of these measurements have consistently supported the popular belief of Anglo intellectual superiority (Kamin, 1974). One group of psychologists led by Louis Terman (1923, 1924) in the early twentieth century went so far as to propose that those Anglos who were rated as superior on intellectual tests should be trained to become the leaders, the philosopher-kings of American society. In this version of the psychology of limits, ability is fixed at birth, and only a select few have the ability to make a worthwhile contribution to the human race. Psychologists have cooperated with this line of thinking, acting as gate keepers, by devising assessment tests to determine which young people should be selected for the educational opportunities that lead to positions of power, influence, and status in later life.

The study of intimacy, human interdependence, war, aging, and death have largely been avoided. While revolutionary breakthroughs have occurred in psychology, such as the existential movement documenting human vulnerability, aloneness, and alienation and the human potential movement with its aim of helping people become more actualizing, sensitive, loving, caring, and in touch with themselves as total persons, the ultimate outcome of these efforts seems to reinforce the philosophy of individualism. In *The Culture of Narcissism* (1979), Christopher Lasch points out that people use their new-found personal freedom created by these movements as justifications to do their own thing, to become more self-focused, self-indulgent, and openly narcissistic. The flower children of the 1960s who were "greening America" with a new consciousness based on love, concern for others, and inner discovery are now wearing three-piece suits, worrying about their expensive mortgage payments in suburbia, and helping the Reagan administration devise a set of foolproof criteria to distinguish between the needy and the "truly needy."

The Afro-American perspective as the foundation for the psychology of Black folks was largely ignored in the first hundred years of formal psychology, beginning in the last quarter of the nineteenth century and continuing into the 1960s. In the pages of psychology textbooks, Afro-Americans were like Ralph Ellison's *Invisible Man* (1947)—unacknowledged and unseen. When there was a brief mention of Afro-Americans under the generic rubric of Negroes, the emphasis was on deviance, pathology, and abnormality, using descriptive terms such as impulse-ridden, passive-dependent, disorganized, emotionally immature, poor self-image, self-hatred, identity confusion, psycho-sexual conflicts, and cultural deprivation (Jones, 1972). These psychological labels bear a close resemblance to the Samboism image of the Black as the clown, the evil beast, and the noble savage popular in American folklore. The flavor of the Samboism myth in American life was captured by Robert Penn Warren in his description of Sambo as:

> the supine, grateful, humble, irresponsible, unmanly, banjo-picking, servile, grinning, slack-jawed, dependent, slow-witted, humorous, child-loving, childlike, watermelon-stealing, spiritual-singing, blamelessly fornicating, happy-go-lucky, hedonistic, faithful black servitor who sometimes might step out of character long enough to utter folk wisdom or bury the family silver to save it from the Yankees.
>
> Later, North and South, Sambo lived on—in white eyes—as Pullman porter, bootblack, yard boy, sharecropper, waiter, barber, elevator operator, the Three Black Crows and Step-and-Fetchit. Sambo it was said was "just the way niggers are." He was eternal and immutable.[1]

The word *Black* in the Euro-American world view connotes a meaning of sinister, evil, foreboding, dirty, unclean, death, and impending doom, while terms such as blackball, blacklist, black market, black sheep, and blackmail indicate behavior or situations that are unacceptable. The devil is black, the angels are white, whiteness as

---

[1] Robert Warren, *Who Speaks for the Negro?* (New York: Random House Inc. 1965), p.52. Reprinted by permission of Random House, Inc.

the psychological opposite of blackness is the essence of purity, cleanliness, goodliness and beauty (Burgest, 1973).

There are some who would consider psychology's support of the position that Afro-Americans are inferior as a blatant example of scientific racism (Guthrie, 1976). Those who feel that scientific racism is too powerful an indictment of American psychologists might be more comfortable with what Wade Nobles (1977) refers to as errors of transubstantiation. Errors of transubstantiation occur when psychologists and other behavioral scientists use a frame of reference developed out of one cultural experience base and attempt without correction to apply this frame of reference to interpret the behavior of people in another cultural framework. Euro-American psychologists developed a set of theories of human behavior out of a Euro-American cultural framework. When these theories, deemed to be universal, are applied to Black folks who don't fit neatly into the established categories, Euro-American psychologists have historically interpreted the difference between Blacks and whites as deviant behavior, without raising the question of valid differences, inappropriate norms, faculty measuring tools, cultural bias, ethnocentrism, or errors of transubstantiation.

Beginning in the 1930s the small number of early pioneer Black psychologists and graduate students began to speak out against the trend in psychology to label Blacks as pathological, defective, and mentally inferior (Franklin, 1980). They were especially concerned about the results of the intelligence testing movement, which classified Blacks as being significantly below whites in mental abilities and the corollary mulatto hypothesis, which stated that the more white blood a Black person had the more intelligent he or she would be. The efforts of this lonely band of brothers and sisters to confront the scientific racism in psychology is chronicled in Dr. Robert Guthrie's book, aptly titled *Even the Rat was White* (1976). The semantics of Guthrie's title refers to the fact that the profession of psychology was so lily-white that even the rats used for laboratory experiments were white. The efforts of these early Black psychologists were of no avail. The tide of institutionalized racism in psychology was too strong and their numbers were too few. Guthrie could find a total of only thirty-two doctorates in psychology and educational psychology awarded to Blacks by American universities between 1920 and 1950. In figures he reports, taken from the American Psychological Association Committee on Equal Opportunity in Psychology, of the 3,767 Ph.D.'s granted between 1920 and 1966 by the ten most prestigious psychology departments in the United States, there were only 8 Blacks. Six of these psychology departments did not grant a single Ph.D. to a Black person. The voice of Blackness in psychology was not to be heard until the 1960s.

THE DEVELOPMENT OF BLACK PSYCHOLOGY—THE MODERN ERA

The modern era of Black psychologists begins in 1968 with the formation of the Association of Black Psychologists (AB Psi). Graduate schools in psychology were still turning out a combined national total of only three or four Black Ph.D.'s in psychology a year. Some major departments of psychology at this late date had not produced a single Black, Ph.D. psychologist. The grand total of psychologists among the more than ten thousand members of the American Psychological Association (APA), psychology's most prestigious organization, was less than 1 percent. At the annual convention of APA in San Francisco in September 1968, approximately fifty-eight Black psychologist delegates and their guests came together to give form and substance to the idea of a national organization of Black psychologists.

This same year, 1968, was the year when the Reverend Dr. Martin Luther King, Jr., was assassinated by a high-powered rifle in Memphis, Tennessee, where he was actively supporting a group of Black garbage collectors in their strike for higher wages, better working conditions, and employee benefits. Many of the Black psychologists who served as founding members of AB Psi in that memorable year were themselves social activists who understood Dr. King's declaration that the basic human issue in this decade of Black revolution was the issue of somebodyness (Lewis, 1970). The driving force behind the civil rights demonstrations of the 1960s and the subsequent strict revolts was a need to confront psychological questions involving liberation, self-determination, Black pride, consciousness of one's worth as a human being, and the right of Black people to determine their own identity. Black people were tired of being invisible, tired of racist stereotypes, tired of being defined inaccurately by behavioral scientists, tired of ineffective social programs based on faulty models, and tired of the choices for the direction of their lives being defined by an oppressive White power structure.

The group of Black psychologists who came together knew about the needs, aspirations, and goals of Blacks from direct experience. They had grown up in the oral tradition of the Black community as sons and daughters of working class, marginally employed, and underemployed shoeshine boys, maids, janitors, waiters, beauty operators, numbers runners, nonunion cooks, all-purpose laborers, and jack-leg preachers. Having received their graduate and professional training in the traditional theories of psychology, they were well aware of the flaws in the white person's logic when it came to offering deficit-oriented psychological explanations about the behavior of Blacks. With their combination of direct experience obtained by growing up in the Black community and academic training in the basic models of psychology, these Black psychologists were uniquely qualified to formulate the theoretical principles and applied direction of Black psychology. They did not discover Black psychology. Black psychology is as old as African heritage and the cultural complexion Blacks have sustained within the American society. The job of Black psychologists was to articulate in psychological terms what was already present in the Black experience.

In a series of papers written in the late 1960s and early 1970s and edited by Reginald Jones in *Black Psychology* (1972), Black psychologists laid out the requirements for conceptual models in the field of Black psychology and the strategies to implement these models: First, the conceptual framework of Black psychology designed to organize, explain, and understand behavior should be developed out of the authentic experience base of Afro-Americans. It is not possible to explain adequately the behavior of Blacks using psychological and conceptual frameworks that have been developed out of the experience base of Euro-Americans (White, 1970). A corollary requirement is that complex mentalistic explanations of Black behavior should be avoided when a more straight-forward observational cause–effect sequence derived from a Black experiential-phenomenal perspective will suffice. If it is a documented fact that the opportunities for Blacks to advance in a particular career field to positions of team leader, foreman, shop manager, middle management, and senior executive range from few to none, as was the case until the late 1960s in the auto industry, high levels of Black absenteeism on Mondays and Fridays should not be explained away by resorting to elaborate theories of motivation deficits and laziness (Hayes, 1980). Second, the psychology of Blackness should concentrate on the strengths Black folks have used to survive, revitalize, actualize, and keep on keepin' on under the oppressive conditions of American life. There has been too much emphasis in psychology on deficit-deficiency models in the past. Third, the search for truth should not be limited to narrow, statistical criteria only. Consensual validation, oral history, intuitiveness, and the word of the people as witnesses of their own direct experience should all be considered as legitimate evidence.

Finally, Black psychologists adopted a posture of social and political advocacy. Our white colleagues in psychology maintained that they were objective scientists whose research findings were politically neutral. Yet, somehow their findings, which were used to formulate public policies such as benign neglect and compensatory education, defined Black people from a point of view that concentrated on defectiveness and pathology. Black psychologists have been honest from the "git'-go, we are pro-Black," actively interested in the psychological well-being of Blacks, and willing to speak out against those social programs, research paradigms, and theoretical formulations that have a potentially oppressive effect on Blacks, while at the same time trying to implement those psychological models and social programs that we feel will improve the quality of life in the Black community.

In the fourteen years since its formal beginning in 1968, Black psychology has established its presence across several areas of psychology. The impact of the efforts of Black psychologists have been felt in community mental health, education, intelligence and ability testing, professional training, forensic psychology, and criminal justice. Black psychologists have presented their findings at professional conferences, legislative hearings, and social policy-making task forces; they have served as expert witnesses in class action suits designed to make institutional policy more responsive to the needs of Black folks. Here are a few of the highlights.

The Larry P. class action suit is the most widely publicized court case brought about by the efforts of Black psychologists. In 1979, after seven years of litigation, the presiding judge declared a permanent ban on the use of standardized intelligence tests as the primary criterion for placing Black and other minority children in classes for the mentally retarded in the state of California. On the basis of critical testimony provided by Black psychologists, Judge Peckam ruled that it was injurious to the mental health of Black children and their families and also a violation of their equal protection rights under the Fourteenth Amendment for them to be labeled as retarded on the basis of culturally biased intelligence tests and placed in classes for the retarded (Hager, 1979). This case will be reviewed more extensively in Chapter Five. Black psychologists were an instrumental part of the planning and follow-up of a prestigious national conference on Patterns of Professional Training in Psychology, conjointly sponsored by the National Institute of Mental Health and the American Psychological Association in 1973 at Vail, Colorado (Korman, 1976). The conference accepted their recommendations regarding changes in graduate admissions policies to increase the number of Black psychologists and their recommendations for changes in graduate education designed to make psychologists of the future more aware of ethnicity and cultural differences as legitimate correlates of behavior. At the time of this writing, the California Psychology Examining Committee (PEC), the state board responsible for regulating and licensing California's 5,400 psychologists, is holding hearings to consider preparation in ethnic psychology not only as a requirement for initial licensure as a psychologist but also as a continuing educational requirement for licensure renewal. This effort was initiated by a Black psychologist, Dr. Thomas Hilliard, who appeared before the Psychology Examining Committee on the recommendation of Dr. Joseph White, another Black psychologist who is the chairman of the PEC. Since California is regarded as the bellwether state, changes that occur in requiring preparation in ethnic psychology are likely to be adopted by other states and graduate education programs in psychology.

In order to disseminate information, announcements, research findings and theoretical papers, the Association of Black Psychologists publishes a newsletter and the *Journal of Black Psychology*. The original edition of *Black Psychology* (Jones, 1972) has been revised (Jones, 1980), and papers by Black psychologists have appeared in a wide variety of professional journals. There are local chapters of AB Psi in nearly every metropolitan area of the country. Annual meetings, separate from the American Psychological Association, are held once a year with an attendance of approximately five hundred Black psychologists and guests. Although the number of Black psychologists and Black graduate students in psychology has shown a steady increase since 1968, Black psychologists still make up less than 3 percent nationally of the Ph.D.'s in psychology. This information is not provided as an exhaustive history, but it is hoped that it will give the reader some idea of the range of activities of Black psychologists.

THE PLAN OF THE BOOK

The synopsis of the basic dimensions of Black psychology—openness, interdependence, tragedy and resilience, the oral tradition, creative synthesis, and the value of direct experience—introduced in Chapter One will be expanded in Chapter Two with a review of the major themes in Black oral literature and language. The objective of the next four chapters is to examine how the primary dimensions of Black psychology are expressed in the Black family (Chapter Three), child development (Chapter Four), teaching (Chapter Five), and learning and mental health (Chapter Six). In each chapter an attempt will be made to compare and contrast the strength-oriented model presented by Black psychologists to the deficit-deficiency model offered by Euro-American psychologists. The terms *Black* and *Afro-American* will be used interchangeably to refer to the target population, Americans of color whose ancestors came from Africa. The author has tried to use the language of the people being written about where it seemed appropriate to reflect the feeling, tone, conceptual style, and expressive flavor of Afro-American life. For those who are uninitiated in the language of soul folks, a glossary of Black sociolinguistic terminology appears in the

Appendix. The book will close with the thesis that the Black psychological ethos is becoming incorporated into the behavior, values, and psychological theory of America's white folks as they struggle with the issues of realness, connectedness, death, loss and tragedy, changing concepts of child development, and alternative family structures. Suggestions for further research include analyses of the relationship between Afro-America life styles and socioeconomic class, the effect of urbanization on Black values, and the impact of the Black social revolution on Black identity and aspirations.

REFERENCES

ARIES, PHILIPPE. *The Hour of Our Death.* New York: Knopf, 1980.

BALDWIN, JAMES. *Notes of a Native Son.* New York: Beacon Press, 1955.

———. *The First Next Time.* New York: Dial Press, 1963.

———. *Going to Meet the Man.* New York: Dial Press, 1965.

BLASSINGAME, JOHN. *The Slave Community.* New York: Oxford University Press, 1972.

BURGEST, ROBERT. "The Racist Use of the English Language," *The Black Scholar,* September 1973, pp. 37–45.

COMER, JAMES. "White Racism: Its Root, Form and Function," *American Journal of Psychiatry,* 126 (1969), 802–806.

CROSS, WILLIAM. "The Negro-to-Black Conversion Experience: Toward a Psychology of Black Liberation," *Black World,* 20, no. 9 July 1971, 13–27.

———. "Models of Nigrescence: A Literature Review," pp. 81–98 in Reginald Jones, *Black Psychology* (2nd ed.). New York: Harper & Row, 1980.

ELKINS, STANLEY. *Slavery, A Problem in America's Institutional and Intellectual Life.* Chicago: University of Chicago Press, 1959.

ELLISON, RALPH. *Invisible Man.* New York: Random House, 1947.

———. *Shadow and Act.* New York: Random House, 1964.

FRANKLIN, VINCENT. "Black Social Scientists and the Mental Testing Movement," in Reginald Jones, *Black Psychology* (2nd ed.). New York: Harper & Row, 1980.

FRAZIER, E. FRANKLIN. *Black Bourgeoisie.* New York: Crowell, Collier & Macmillan, 1962.

FREDRICKSON, GEORGE. "The Gutman Report," *The New York Review,* September 30, 1976, pp. 18–22, 27.

FREUD, SIGMUND. *Civilization and Its Discontents.* Standard Edition. London: Hogarth Press, 1961; originally published 1930, Vol. 20.

———. *The Ego and the Id.* Standard Edition. London: Hogarth Press, 1961; originally published 1923, Vol. 19.

Guthrie, Robert. *Even the Rat Was White: A Historical View of Psychology.* New York: Harper & Row, 1976.

———. "The Psychology of Black Americans: An Historical Perspective," in Reginald Jones, ed., *Black Psychology* (2nd ed.). New York: Harper & Row, 1980.

GUTMAN, HERBERT. *The Black Family in Slavery and Freedom, 1750– 1925.* New York: Vintage Books, 1976.

HAGER, PHILLIP. "IQ Testing to Place Pupils in Retarded Classes Banned," *Los Angeles Times,* October 17, 1979, pp. 1, 21.

HARE, NATHAN. *Black Anglo Saxons.* New York: Mangani & Mansell, 1965.

HAYES, WILLIAM. "Radical Black Behaviorism," in Reginald Jones, *Black Psychology* (2nd ed.). New York: Harper & Row, 1980.

HUGHES, LANGSTON. *The Ways of White Folks.* New York: Knopf, 1934.

———. *The Best of Simple.* New York: Hill & Wang, 1961.

———. *Selected Poems.* New York: Knopf, 1965.

JEFFERS, LANCE. "Afro-American Literature: The Conscience of Man," *The Black Scholar,* January 1971, pp. 47–53.

JONES, REGINALD. *Black Psychology* (1st ed.). New York: Harper & Row, 1972.

———. *Black Psychology* (2nd ed.) New York: Harper & Row, 1980.

KAMIN, LEON. *The Science and Politics of IQ.* New York: John Wiley, 1974.

KORMAN, MAURICE, ed. *Levels and Patterns of Professional Training in Psychology.* Washington, D.C.: American Psychological Association, 1976.

LASCH, CHRISTOPHER. *The Culture of Narcissism: American Life in An Age of Diminishing Expectations.* New York: W.W. Norton & Co., 1979.

LEWIS, DAVID. *King: A Critical Biography*. New York: Penguin Books, 1970.

MALCOLM X (with the assistance of ALEX HALEY). *The Autobiography of Malcolm X*. New York: Grove Press, 1966.

MBITI. J. S. *African Religions and Philosophies*. Garden City, N.Y.: Doubleday, Anchor Books, 1970.

NOBLES, WADE. "African Philosophy: Foundation for Black Psychology," pp. 18–32 in Reginald Jones, *Black Psychology* (1st ed.). New York: Harper & Row, 1972.

————. "Africanity: Its Role in Black Families," *The Black Scholar*, June 1974, pp. 10–17.

————. "Black People in White Insanity, an Issue for Community Mental Health," *Journal of Afro-American*, 4, no. 1, (Winter 1976), 21–27.

————. "The Rhythmic Impulse: The Issue of Africanity in Black Family Dynamics." Paper presented to the Second Annual Symposium on Black Psychology, Black Students Psychology Association, and Department of Psychology, Ann Arbor, Mich., April 1977.

————. "Toward an Empirical and Theoretical Framework for Defining Black Families," *Journal of Marriage and the Family*, November 1978, pp. 679–688.

RAWICK, GEORGE. *From Sundown to Sunup: The Making of the Black Community*. Westport, Conn.: Greenwood Publishing Co., 1972.

SHOSTROM, EVERETT. *Man, the Manipulator*. Nashville: Abingdon Press, 1967.

SMITH, ADAM. *Wealth of Nations* (2nd ed.). Oxford: Clarendon Press, 1880.

SMITHERMAN, GENEVA. *Talkin and Testifyin: The Language of Black America*. Boston: Houghton Mifflin, 1977.

STAPLES, ROBERT. *Introduction to Black Sociology*. New York: McGraw-Hill, 1976.

TERMAN, LEWIS. *Intelligence Tests and School Reorganization*. New York: World Book Co., 1923.

————. "The Conservation of Talent," *School and Society*, 19, no. 483 (March 1924), 363.

THOMAS, CHARLES. "Different Strokes for Different Folks," *Psychology Today*, 4, no. 4 (1970), 48–53, 78–80.

——. *Boys No More.* Beverly Hills: Glencoe Press, 1971.

WARREN, ROBERT. *Who Speaks for the Negro?* New York: Random House, Inc. 1965.

WASHINGTON, E. DAVIDSON. *Selected Speeches of Booker T. Washington.* New York, 1932; reprinted 1976. New York: Kraus Reprints Co.

WHITE, JOSEPH. "Toward a Black Psychology," *Ebony,* September 1970, pp. 44–45, 48–50, 52.

WILLIAMS, ROBERT. "The Problem of Match and Mismatch in Testing Black Children," pp. 67–75 in L. Miller, ed., *The Testing of Black Children.* Englewood Cliffs, N.J.: Prentice-Hall, 1974.

WILLIAMS, ROBERT, ed. *Ebonics, the True Language of Black Folks.* St. Louis: Institute of Black Studies, 1975.

WRIGHT, RICHARD. *Native Son.* New York: Harper & Row, 1964.

——. *Black Boy.* New York: Harper & Row, 1966.

CHAPTER TWO

PSYCHOLOGICAL THEMES IN BLACK LANGUAGE, ORAL LITERATURE, AND EXPRESSIVE PATTERNS

INTRODUCTION

Six recurring psychological themes can be identified in the language, oral literature, and expressive patterns of Black folks: (1) emotional vitality, (2) realness, (3) resilience, (4) interrelatedness, (5) the value of direct experience, (6) distrust and deception. These themes symbolizing the affective, cognitive, and cultural flavor of the Black psychological perspective will be discussed in this chapter.

VITALITY

There is a sense of aliveness, animation, emotional vitality, and openness to feelings expressed in the language, oral literature, song, dance (sometimes called the poetry of motion), body language, folk poetry, and expressive thought of Black folks (Redmond, 1971). Black dance and oral literature are described by Jeffers (1971) as being vivacious, exuberant, sensuous, and wholesomely uninhibited, a statement that life should abound and flourish with the vigorous intensity of the Funky Chicken rather than the sedateness of the waltz or fox trot. In the Black oral tradition the act of speaking is a performance on the stage of life (Holt, 1975). To capture and hold the attention of the listener, the speaker is expected to make words come alive, to use ear-filling phrases that stir the imagination with heavy reliance on tonal rhymes, symbolism, figures of speech, and personification. The vitality expressed in Black language is life-affirming; despair, apathy, and downtroddenness are rejected. Feelings are not suppressed, but freely shared with others. The speaker, performer, preacher, or singer touches the collective experience base of the listeners by being honest and authentic, telling about life as it really is.

REALNESS—TELLIN' IT LIKE IT IS

The message expressed in the folk poetry of the blues and gospel music is that profound sorrow, pain, hardship, and struggle cannot be avoided. The blues singer opens up the window of his or her soul and tells it like it 'tis. Life does not play with Black folks. Disappointment, tragedy, setbacks, and defeat are inevitable. There are dues to be paid, nobody gets away clean. This is simply the way things are (Neal, 1972). The first step of learning to survive is to see life exactly as it is, without self-deception or romantic pieties. The story of the blues and gospel lyrics is not, however, one of resignation or despair. In the Black ethos tragedy, defeat and disappointment are not equated with psychological destruction. The goal of a Black presence in the face of tragedy is to keep on keepin' on, to keep the faith, to maintain a cool steadiness, and to keep on climbin' until one has transcended. Langston Hughes conveys the steadiness, persistence, and toughness of Black folks in the face of hardship in his poem, "Mother to Son," where an aging Black mother is breaking down the facts of life she has learned through experience to her young son. She sums it up by telling him:

Life for me ain't been no crystal stair.
It's had tacks in it,
And splinters,
And boards torn up,
And places with no carpet on the floor—
Bare.
But all the time

> *I'se been a-climbin' on*
> *And reachin' landin's,*
> *And turnin' corners*
> *And sometimes goin' in the dark*
> *Where there ain't been no light.*
> *So boy, don't you turn your back.*
> *Don't you set down on the steps*
> *'Cause you finds it kinder hard.*
> *Don't you fall now—*
> *For I'se still goin', honey,*
> *I'se still climbin',*
> *And life for me ain't been no crystal stair."*[1]

Gladys Knight (1973), a modern-day blues and rhythm singer, describes Black presence in the face of tragedy as being a situation where "I've got to use my imagination to make the best of a bad situation to keep on keepin' on."[2]

Psychological growth and emotional maturity cannot be completed until the person has paid his or her dues by overcoming hardship, defeat, sorrow, and grief (Baldwin, 1963). The person who has come through the storm is no longer afraid and his or her soul may look back and wonder how they made it over the troubled sea of life. He or she has a healthy respect for life, is not afraid to be real, authentic, or genuine, is aware of his or her own vulnerability and has the capacity to be compassionate and emphatic with the the struggles of others.

RESILIENCE AND REVITALIZATION

The picture of human existence presented by the "Blues People" (Jones, 1963) and the gospel artists goes beyond oppression, hardship, and struggle. There is more to life than unrequited love, two-timing women, unbearable sorrow, and run-down neighborhoods. On the other side of the ledger to balance the emotional and psychological spectrum are the renewal experiences of senuousness,

---

[1]Copyright 1926 by Alfred A Knopf, Inc. and renewed 1954 by Langston Hughes. Reprinted from *Selected Poems of Langston Hughes*, by Langston Hughes, by permission of the publisher.

[2]Appears on "I've Got to Use My Imagination" album by Gladys Knight (1973).

joy, and laughter. The trouble will pass, the blues won't last always, and freedom will emerge on some bright sunshiny day.

The consciousness of pain, sorrow, and hurt in blues and gospel music is not accompanied by feelings of guilt, shame, and self-rejection. It is a pure sadness that can be differentiated from the clinical syndrome of depression where guilt, shame, and anger transformed into self-depreciation work against the serenity of sadness. The openness to a balanced spectrum of human emotions in Black consciousness unencumbered by guilt, shame, and self-debasement makes it easier to draw upon the revitalization powers of sensuousness, joy, and laughter. The blues singer, despite the pain of loss, grief, and defeat, is fully aware of the excitement and euphoria of sensuality; he or she knows that "A good looking woman will make a bull dog gnaw his bone." Reference to the pleasures of sexuality is explicit in the blues with lyrics like "My baby rocks me with one steady roll."[3] If terminal illness prevents one from looking forward to future renewal experiences through sensuality, then one can look back with the satisfaction that "I have had my fun if I don't get well no more."

Church-going Black folks are open to being moved by the spirit to peak experiences of joy, happiness, and euphoria. Those who erroneously label gospel music as sorrow songs miss the transcendent theme of dark clouds passing, of being bound for higher ground and the joy of being touched by the spirit. The ability to stay in touch with the energizing process generated by the uplifting experiences of feeling good, sensuality, and joy have enabled Black folks to revitalize, keep the faith, keep on keepin' on, and keep on climbin'.

The themes of sensuality and joy in the oral literature of Black folks are complemented by the presence of laughter. Blacks use humor as a weapon to confront adversity (Davis, 1968; Lomax, 1961). One of the primary topics of Black humor historically was the absurdity of racial oppression in a Christian nation. Levine (1977) describes a comical anecdote emphasizing how restrictive southern racial codes forced Black folks to invert their natural inclinations. A Black man accidentally falls from a tall building, suddenly in mid-air

---

[3]Larry Neal, "The Ethos of the Blues," *The Black Scholar*, 1972, pp. 42–48. Reprinted by permission.

he realizes that he is going to land on a White woman. The brother forces himself to reverse direction in mid-air and lands back on top of the building. Black humor expressed by social critics like Godfrey Cambridge (1961) and Richard Pryor (1975) goes right to the heart of troublesome social-political realities while avoiding the inane, slapstick, frivolousness of the Bud Abbott–Lou Costello variety. Tragedy and comedy are juxtaposed so that the same situation simultaneously invokes laughter and tears.

The prototype of realism in Black comedy is Jesse B. Semple, a fictional underemployed urban Black male living in Harlem in the 1940s and 1950s created by Langston Hughes (1950, 1953, and 1957), better known as Simple. Through Jess Simple, Hughes used a sardonic, poignant, gallows-type humor to discuss life in Black America. Simple worked for white folks in a low-status job downtown during the week, and his social commentary on economic conditions, male-female relationships, racial oppression, growing up in the South, Black pride, struggling for survival, and the resiliency of Black folks takes place in Patty's Bar, Simple's favorite after-work hangout. The flavor of Simple's penetrating wit can be captured from the passage below, where Simple, who is recovering from a bout of pneumonia, identifies all the tragedies that can happen to a Black man as he passes through the world. The second person in Simple's narration is an anonymous straight man:

"Not only am I half dead right now from pneumonia, but everyting else *has* happened to me! I have been cut, shot, stabbed, run over, hit by a car, and tromped by a horse. I have been robbed, fooled, deceived, two-timed, double-crossed, dealt seconds, and might near blackmailed—but I am still here."

"You're a tough man," I said.

"I have been fired, laid off, and last week given an indefinite vacation, also Jim Crowed, segregated, barred out, insulted, eliminated, called black, yellow, and red, locked in, locked out, locked up, also left holding the bag. I have been caught in the rain, caught in raids, caught short with my rent, and caught with another man's wife. In my time I have been caught—but I am still here.!"

"You have suffered," I said.

"Suffered!" cried Simple. "My mamma should have named me Job instead of Jess Semple. I have been underfed, underpaid, under-nourished, and everything but *undertaken*. I been bit by dogs, cats, mice, rats, poll parrots, fleas, chiggers, bedbugs, granddaddies, mosquitoes, and a gold-toothed woman."

"Great day in the morning!"

"That ain't all," said Simple. "In this life I been abused, confused, misused, accused, false-arrested, tried, sentenced, paroled, black-jacketed, beat, third-degreed, and near about lynched.'"

"Anyhow, your health has been good—up to now," I said.

"Good health nothing," objected Simple, waving his hands, kicking off the cover, and swinging his feet out of bed. "I done had everything from flat feet to a flat head. Why, man, I was born with measles! Since then I had smallpox, chickenpox, whooping cough, croup, appendicitis, athlete's foot, tonsillitis, arthritis, backache, mumps, and a strain— but I am still here, Daddy-o, I'm still here!"

"Having survived all that, what are you afraid of, now that you are almost over pneumonia?"

"I'm afraid," said Simple, "I will die before my time."[4]

The willingness to laugh in the face of misfortune without denying the seriousness of adverse reality is part of the survival equipment of Afro-Americans. Humor grounded in reality is psychologically refreshing; it defines the situation in manageable terms and prevents the build-up of unbearable anxieties by not allowing people to take themselves too seriously. Soul is the ability to laugh while growing with hardships, paying dues, and transcending tragedies.

The power of the words of blues singers, folk poets, comedians, and preachers to uplift, heal, inspire, and revitalize comes in large measure from their adeptness in reaching out to touch others with messages from a shared pool of experiences that both speaker

[4]Reprinted by permission of Harold Ober Associates Incorporated. Copyright © 1950 by Langston Hughes. Renewed 1978 by George H. Bass as Executor for the Estate of Langston Hughes.

and listener can bear witness to. In the act of touching others through a shared experienced frame, the individuals know that they are not alone, that they are psychologically connected to others who can affirm the actuality of their experiences. In the Black church the preacher physically touches the parishioner with the "laying of the hands" in the presence of others to symbolize that the person being touched has not been spiritually forsaken or abandoned. In *The Fire Next Time,* Baldwin describes the psychological impact of sharing, witnessing, closeness, embracing, and affirmation from his days as a teenage preacher in a Harlem storefront church. During an adolescent identity crisis Baldwin fell to the floor of the church in a fit of guilt-induced panic. While he was on the floor all night, the church members rejoiced and prayed "over me to bring me through, and in the morning they raised me and told me I was saved." Baldwin goes on to describe the drama and excitement he felt when the church came together in one harmonious voice:

> There is no music like that music, no drama like the drama of saints rejoicing, the sinners moaning, the tambourines racing, and all those voices coming together and crying holy unto the Lord. There is still, for me, no pathos quite like the pathos of those multicolored, worn, somehow triumphant and transfigured faces, speaking from the depths of a visible, tangible, continuing despair of the goodness of the Lord. I have never seen anything to equal the fire and excitement that sometimes, without warning, fill a church, causing the church, as Leadbelly and so many others have testified, to "rock." Nothing that has happend to me since equals the power and the glory that I sometimes felt when, in the middle of a sermon, I knew I was somehow, by some miracle really carrying, as they said, "the Word"—when the Church and I were one. Their pain and their joy were mine, and mine were theirs—they surrendered their pain and joy to me, I surrendered mine to them—and their cries of "Amen!" and "Hallelujah!" and "Yes, Lord." and "Praise His Name!" and "Preach It, brother!" sustained and whipped on my solos until we all became equal, wringing wet, singing and dancing, in anguish and rejoicing, at the foot of the altar."[5]

[5]James Baldwin, *The Fire Next Time.* Copyright © 1963, 1962 by James Baldwin. Permission granted by The Dial Press and Michael Joseph Ltd.

INTERDEPENDENCE, INTERRELATEDNESS, CONNECTEDNESS, AND SYNTHESIS

In the theoretical model of Black psychology presented by Wade Nobles (1976) interrelatedness, connectedness, and interdependence are viewed as the unifying philosophic concepts in the Afro-American experience base. Interrelatedness, connectedness, and interdependence are prominent themes in Black language with respect to the interactive dynamics between speaker and listener, the power of words to control, cognitive style, timing, and communicative competence. The spoken word in the Black community is the pervasive force that connects human experiences. Human contact, the connecting linkage between people, is established by the spoken word. Through the spoken word linkages are established across time and space, transmitting the Afro-American heritage from one generation to another.

The language of soul folks, whether it occurs on street corners, in beauty shops, barber shops, parties, love raps, playgrounds, or in political speeches and church sermons, is charcterized by the interrelatedness of speaker and listener. The act of speaking is a dramatic presentation of one's personhood to those who share a background of similar acculturation (Holt, 1975). The listener acts as an echo chamber, repeating, cosigning, validating, and affirming the message of the speaker with amens, right-ons, yes sirs, teach-ons, and you aint' never lied's. The speaker sends out a call and the listener responds. During this call–response dialogue, the speaker and listener are joined together in a common psycholinguistic space. Each participant has the opportunity to expand the message through amplification and repetition. Spillers (1971) illustrates the interactive interchange between speaker and listener by recalling a sermon and the accompanying Amen corner from her childhood that went something like this:

PREACHER:	The same Christ, the same man.
CONGREGATION:	Same man.

PREACHER:	Who sits high and looks low, who rounded the world in the middle of his hands.
CONGREGATION:	Middle of his hands.
PREACHER:	The same man who fed 5,000 and still had some left over.
CONGREGATION:	Yes sir! Had some left.
PREACHER:	The same man who raised the dead and who walked the waters and calmed the seas.
CONGREGATION:	Let's hold him up church.
PREACHER:	This same man is looking out for you and me.[6]

The Black speaker establishes a form of situational control vis-a-vis the listener by defining a reality using vivid imagery drawn from a body of collective experiences that others understand and can relate to events in their life space (Holt, 1975). The speaker controls the situation linguistically with words that touch the psychoaffective rhythms, activating emotions of joy, laughter, sadness, strength, optimism, and feelings that power and control over Black destiny by Black people in a racist society can become a reality. Describing the collective experience of oppression with tonal rhymes like "we have been abused, misused, refused and confused," Black speakers draw a picture of reality that their listeners can cosign and affirm. Martin Luther King, Jr., used metaphors to describe the reality that Black people were not satisfied with the slow pace of the civil rights legislation in August of 1963 and we would not be satisfied until "Justice rolls down like water and righteousness like a mighty stream."[7] When Stokely Carmichael used the term *Black power,* Black folks intuitively knew that he meant Black folks must control the reality of what was going down in their community. Later, he wrote a book on Black power (1967) to explain what he meant so White folks could understand.

The extensive use of metaphor in Black speech reflects a cognitive style where likeness, correspondence, similarity, and analogous relationships between ideas, events, and concepts are shown by using picturesque imagery that appeals conjointly to the intellect

[6]Hortense Spillers, "Martin Luther King and The Style of The Black Sermon," *The Black Scholar,* September 1971, pp. 14–27. Reprinted by permission.
[7]From "I Have a Dream" by Martin Luther King, Jr. Copyright © 1963 by Martin Luther King, Jr. Reprinted by permission of Joan Daves.

and emotions. Inner-city youth speak of successful sexual encounters as "hitting the jill pot" (Holt, 1975). King (1963) paints a picture comparing the exhausting struggle against the evil consequences of oppression as having left people "battered by the storms of persecution and staggered by the winds of police brutality."[8] The metaphor in this case creates an analogous relationship between the evils of Jim Crow justice and being "battered by the storms and staggered by the winds."

In Black speech the words come alive through colorful poetic sketches that arouse feelings. The speaker uses visual symbols to draw a picture of what's happening. The intellectual meaning is carried by implication creating a psychoaffective or cognitive-affective synthesis (Smitherman, 1977). Holt captures the cognitive-affective syntheses in the visual imagery expressed by Black youth in the following statements:

- "getten over like a fat rat in a cheese factory"
- that aint nothing man, ice it
- higher than nine kites on a breezy day
- man that dude was really stroking
- just as cool as she wanted to be
- I don't know what page you on
- you on the wrong channel, tune in
- "Jim he was faking it and making it
- I'm gonna put your hip boots on
- Lay out till you get wired up
- Layin on the cut till I'm hipped
- Freeze that shit and space.[9]

The metaphor in Black language is a teaching device (Spillers, 1971). Speakers depend on the common background between themselves and their listeners to establish impact and associate meanings to the words. Presentational symbols in the form of visual imagery are substituted for abstract concepts to expand and clarify meanings from an Afro-American cultural perspective. Picturesque

---

[8]Ibid
[9]Grace Holt, "Metaphor, Black Discourse Style and Cultural Reality," in R.L. Williams (ed.), *Ebonics, The True Language of Black Folks*. (St. Louis: Institute of Black Studies, 1975), p. 87

imagery stimulates the power of the mind to see, to visualize abstract relationships, and to project novel interpretations (Holt, 1975).

Black metaphoric expressions generate multiple meanings. The cultural connotation is conveyed by translating the expression or figure of speech through an ethnotropic filter delineated by an Afro-American world view. The specific meaning of a statement in a given situation is dependent on contextual cues, coupled with the cultural sophistication and innovativeness of the participants. "Going to meet the man," a folk expression widely used in the Black community, with "the man" symbolizing a white male in authority (who generally ain't given the brothers and sisters no slack) can be interpreted to mean going downtown to work in a menial job, going to court to deal with a recalcitrant judge, going to the finance company to explain why the car payment is late, plus a host of other interpretations contingent on the situation. *Going to Meet the Man* is the title of a book of essays by James Baldwin (1965). In one of the essays, the dying era of blatant southern racism is symbolized by "the man," a white southern sheriff who allows the armor of his racism to be slowly penetrated by the vitality, resilience, persistence, courage, humanism, and ultimate righteousness of his adversary, a young Black civil rights worker.

Black children learn to use a linguistic style that is saturated with Black folk expressions, ethnotropisms,[10] metaphors, visual imagery, and figures of speech. They cannot easily translate the isolated words and literal meanings of the conventional Euro-American language they study in school into their normal speech patterns, and their teachers will not permit them to use their normal expressive patterns in the classroom. In his autobiography, *Die Nigger Die,* Rap Brown (1969) describes the conflict arising from his verbal competence in Black expressive styles and the expectation of his teachers with respect to learning traditional English poetry. Running it down to another brother, Rap displays his verbal wizardry by telling him:

> *Man you must not know who I am.*
> *I am sweet peeter jeeter, the womb beater.*
> *The baby maker the cradle shaker.*

[10]Ethnotropism is the use of a word, phrase or utterance in a different cultural context for the purpose of giving life or emphasis to an idea (Holt, 1975).

The deer slayer the buck binder the woman finder.
Known from the gold coast to the rocky shores of Maine.
Rap is my name and love is my game.[11]

Rap goes on to say "and the teacher expected me to set up in class and study poetry after I could run down shit like that, if anybody needed to study poetry, she needed to study mine."

The interactive balance between the linguistic rhythms of the speaker and listener characterized by the call–response is synchronized by a reciprocal command of timing and pace. The goal is to be in time with the beat, pulse, tempo, and rhythm of the speech flow. In Martin Luther King's Montgomery speech "We're on the Move," shown in the Montgomery-to-Memphis documentary, an unidentified man stood at King's side repeating the key words, "Yes, suh, we're on the move." The audience picked up the tempo of King's rhythms and reinforced the basic message with the call–response formula:

KING: We can't be dissuaded now.
AUDIENCE: We're on the move.
KING: No wave of racism can stop us now.
AUDIENCE: We're on the move.
KING: Not even the marching of mighty armies can stop us now.
AUDIENCE: We're on the move.

The speaker knows what images, tonal rhythms, metaphors, and stress phrases will generate the interactive sequence because he or she has seen the technique work for others many times (Spillers, 1971). Black adolescents perfect the timing, pace, and rhythm of their language game in peer-group interaction by continuously alternating the roles of speaker and listener in verbal interchanges that require active participation, such as playing the Dozens, signifyin', love rappin', lug droppin', and soundin'.

In the Afro-American world view, concepts of timing, rhythm, pace, and sequence extend beyond the dynamics of language to encompass life, history, and the flow of movement in the universe. Human existence as outlined by King (Lewis, 1971) has a certain repetitive sequence delineated by cycles of oppression, resistance,

[11]H. Rap Brown, *Die Nigger Die.* Copyright © 1969 by Lynn Brown. Permission granted by The Dial Press and Allison & Busby Ltd.

TABLE 2–1

TERMS USED TO DESIGNATE SOCIAL-LINGUISTIC INTERACTION

1. Bad Mouth, Mouthin'	28. Mau Mau, Mauing
2. Base, Basin'	29. Mumblin'
3. Blow, Blow on	30. Pimp Talk
4. Call and Response	31. Protection Talk
5. Cappin'	32. Pull Coat
6. Cop a Plea	33. Rappin'
7. Cop on	34. Rhapsodize
8. Cover snatch, Snatchin'	35. Runnin' It Down
9. Dozens, Dirty Dozens	36. Scat Singin'
10. Drop a Dime	37. Screamin'
11. Fat Lip	38. Showboatin'
12. Fat Mouth, Mouthin'	39. Shuckin' and Jivin'
13. Frontin' Off	40. Signify, Signifyin'
14. Gate Mouth, Mouthin'	41. Soundin'
15. Gibb, Gibbin' (Jibb)	42. Splib Wibbin'
16. Gripp, Grippin'	43. Stuff Playin'
17. Group, Grouped	44. Sweet Mouthin'
18. High Siding	45. Talkin' Proper
19. Hoorah, Hoorahin'	46. Talkin' Shit (Talking Trash)
20. Jaw Jackin'	47. Talkin' in Tongue
21. Jeffin'	48. Tautin'
22. Jivin'	49. Testify-Testifyin'
23. Jonin'	50. Toast, Toastin'
24. Larcen, Larcenin'	51. Tom Tom, Tommin'
25. Lolly Gaggin'	52. Whop, Whoppin' Game
26. Lug Droppin'	53. Woofin', Wolfing
27. Mack, Mackin'	54. Woof (Wolf) Ticket

Adapted from E. Smith "Evolution and Continuing Presence of the Oral Tradition in Black America" (Unpublished Doctoral Dissertation, University of California—Irvine, 1974). Reprinted by permission.

transcendence, and freedom. Time is eternal and freedom for Black folks is just a matter of time. The rule of Yacob, symbolized in Muslim mythology by the mad scientist who created the evil white person, cannot last forever (Malcolm X, 1965). Both a person and a people must know when to make their move, when to hold on, when to cool it, and when to woof. King perceived the time frame of the civil rights movement, triggered in 1955 by the refusal of Rosa Parks to move to the segregated section of a Birmingham, Alabama, bus, as fitting into an historical Zeitgeist of resistance that would be followed by an era of freedom and equality. Eldridge Cleaver (1968) viewed Mrs. Parks's historic act and the freedom struggle it initiated as symbolic of a gear shifting somewhere in the universe.

The importance of the spoken word in the Black community is demonstrated by the large number of linguistic terms used to designate different forms of social-linguistic interaction. A list of fifty-four social-linguistic terms compiled by Smith (1974) appears in Table 2–1. Definitions and examples of appropriate situational usage are presented in the Appendix.

Mastery in the art of skillfully utilizing these social-linguistic categories gives the person access to a wide range of interpersonal interactions, information, and learning situations. The person with a high level of receptive and expressive communicative competence knows how to break it down, how to stay on top of a situation verbally, how to tune in to what others are running down, and when it is appropriate to employ a particular social-linguistic category. The oral tradition is an integral part of Black identity. The emotional, psychological, and cultural tone of the Black ethos is expressed by means of the spoken word. Competence in understanding and interpreting the Black world view as it is communicated by Black oral expressive styles comes about as a result of experiences in living and relating to others.

THE VALUE OF DIRECT EXPERIENCE

There is no substitute in the Black ethos for actual experiences gained in the course of living. The natural facts, eternal truths, wisdom of the ages, and basic percepts of survival emerge from the experiences of life; "you cannot lie to life." In interpersonal relationships, matters of race and the affairs of nations, "the truth will out," no lie can last for long. The truth can stand the test of time and experience; a lie cannot. The slaves kept the faith in the belief that freedom was just a matter of time (how long? not long), the experience of captivity would pass because slavery was against the laws of God and humanity.

A person lacking in mother wit, the common sense of life experiences, who flaunts untested book knowledge is perceived in the Black idiom as an educated fool. Sometimes college brothers and sisters, after a few courses in economic theory and sociology, come home in the summer and expound the theoretical principles of Marxism, Keynesian economics, stagflation, and supply-side economic theory to the community folks. They are usually stopped short by questions about "when do it get me a job?" The *Best and Brightest* of David Halberstam (1971) refused to heed the lessons of the unsuccessful experiences of the French in Vietnam. They went ahead with their elaborate geopolitical theories, computer-based technologies, and body count projections only to get themselves deeper and deeper into a no-win situation. The brothers on the corner, without the benefit of computer-based technology and elaborate geopolitical theory said from the gate that "you ain't got no business puttin' your foot on another man's land." Time and experience proved them right.

The collective lessons of experience are carried forward from one generation to the next by the oral tradition. Children are taught the percepts of life through a vast oral literature consisting of parables, folk verses, folk tales, biblical verses, songs, and proverbs. Many older Black adults can remember hearing these sayings from their parents and grandparents.

- The truth will out.
- Don't sign no checks with your mouth that your ass can't cash.
- Hard head make a soft behind.
- You better be yourself or you gonna be by yourself.
- One monkey don't stop no show.
- Only a fool plays the golden rule in a crowd that don't play fair.
- If you lay down with dogs you gonna come up with fleas.
- What goes around, comes around.
- You better learn how to work before work works you.
- You don't git to be old being no fool.

Each generation has to refashion and expand the meaning of the proverbial wisdom to encompass the events of their time and place. In a moment of deep contemplation during a Harlem racial riot a few hours after his father's funeral, James Baldwin (1955) found himself reflecting on the meaning of life contained in his father's parables, sermons, and verses. Like many adolescents and young adults, he had come to the conclusion that the values represented in the collective experience of his father's dictums were meaningless. Now, in the hour of his father's death, amidst the destruction going on around him, Baldwin saw the familiar texts and songs arranged before him like empty bottles "waiting to hold the meaning which life would give them for me."[12] Since that time Baldwin has filled the empty bottles with his own experiences combined with a more mature understanding of the collective ethos transmitted by his father. Utilizing his "gift of tongues" (Warren, 1965), Baldwin has gone on to articulate and enlarge on the Black world view. In a series of articles, plays, essays, and novels, Baldwin has carried the word forth to the next generation. This is his legacy; nothing is ever escaped, dues must be paid, tragedy is necessary for personal growth, and revitalization of the human spirit comes about through love, sensuousness, joy, and laughter.

The notion of psychological growth arising from discoveries initiated by life experiences is evident in the autobiographies of Richard Wright (1945, 1977) and Malcolm X (1965). Richard Wright started out believing in the Protestant ethic of hard work, self-control, personal initiative, resourcefulness, and future planning, only to discover the pervasiveness of structural racism in America, both North and South. His determination to write about life in Black America exactly as he experienced it, with racism as a more prevailing force than economic class, provided him with the motivation to keep on climbin' and ultimately caused the demise of his flirtation with the Communist party.

Malcolm X goes through several transitions as he progresses experientially from a child in a nearly all-white farming community

---

[12]Baldwin, James. *Notes of a Native Son.* Boston: Beacon Press, 1955.

of the Midwest to his ultimate break with the Lost Found Nation of Islam. After being discouraged from considering a career in law by his white elementary school teacher, Malcolm X moved on to brief tenures in the Negro jobs of that day in Boston and New York; shoeshine boy, coach boy on the railroads, and waiter. Subsequently, as a young adult he drifted into street hustling, petty crime, and burglary, which landed him in prison. In prison he embraced the faith of the Black Muslim Nation of Islam, and after his release became an activist under the tutelage of his father figure, mentor, and role model Elija Muhammad. During his experience as an activist minister he discovered that the narrow religious band of nationalism espoused by the Nation of Islam was too confining to produce the changes in America necessary to bring about a wider range of choices for Black folks. He became convinced by the dictates of his own experience that in order to consolidate his identity and generate a broader platform of social change, it would be necessary for him to seek his independence from the Nation of Islam.

The relationship between identity and life experiences comes together in Ralph Ellison's *Invisible Man* (1952). The invisible man, the protagonist without a name to symbolize the invisible presence of Black people in the mainstream of American life, goes through a series of transformations before he discovers that attempts to avoid coming to grips with the struggle to define who he really is by becoming a carbon copy of someone else are doomed to fail. As a college student and later as a social activist, with time in between spent as an angry rebel, the protagonist tries to become a facsimile of his mentors, only to feel disillusioned and betrayed when he finds out that his role models are not what they appear to be. Sitting alone in a cellar at the end of the novel, he gradually comes to the unavoidable conclusion that nothing is ever escaped. He painfully discovers that in order to achieve his identity he can no longer become a duplicate of someone else, he must confront his existence and take the responsibility for sorting things out by listening to the internal voice of his experience.

Older people in the Black community are the reservoirs of the wisdom accumulated during the experiences of a lifetime. They are the storehouses of the oral tradition and the keepers of the heritage.

The elderly are valued because they have been through the experiences that can only come with age. They have been "down the line," as the saying goes, seen the comings and goings of life, and been through the repetitive cycles of oppression, struggle, survival, backlash, and renewed struggle. Older people have stood the test of time and adversity, paid their dues, transcended tragedy, and learned how to keep on keepin' on. According to Richard Pryor, "You learn something when you listen to old people, they ain't all fools cause you don't git to be old bein' no fool, lotta young wise men deader than a motherfucker!"[13] The presence of older people provides a seasoned steadiness during troubled times in the Black extended family. Bill Withers (1971) in a song "Grandma's Hands," sings about the soothing impact Black grandmothers have on troubled young adults and the comforting effect of their affection on children.

In the *Children of Ham,* Claude Brown (1973) presents a quasi-fictive group of Harlem teenagers who have banded together in an extended family. They live in abandoned tenement buildings and survive the dangers of the streets by mutual support, mother wit, and resourcefulness. One of the young women, Dee Dee, takes up fortune telling, a money-making business in Harlem. Women get together in homes and beauty parlors on Saturday nights for tea-leaf and palm-reading parties fortified with pots of pigs feet, neck bones, and collard greens. Dee Dee has checked out the whole gamut of tea-leaf reading, roots, horoscopes, astrology, tarot cards, clairvoyance, and soothsaying. She found out, however, that the clientele won't trust her with their innermost secrets because she is too young to have been around long enough to know what life is all about. Dee Dee, who is also into drama, is trying to figure out how to convey the appearance of age by acting the part of an older woman. She thinks that if she can create the impression of being an older woman her customers will feel confident that she has the requisite experiences to render sound advice. Dee Dee considers getting a way out name like Madam Zooloo or Sister Buzzard, wearing a wig, changing her manner of dress, learning to walk differently, slowing

[13]Appears in "Mudbone" from the album *Richard Pryor: Is It Something I Said?* (New York: Reprise Records, 1975). Reprinted by permission.

down the movements of her hands, not turning too fast, and decreasing the level of her pep and energy, because when people get old they naturally slow down.

There are periodic reports that the white elderly feel abandoned, useless, alone, and terrified by the prospect of death (Clark and Gosnell, 1977). Old Black folks, on the other hand, are an integral part of the community. They are resilient, know how to survive, get over, get down, socialize, and do the old-folks romance with members of the opposite sex. The Black elderly have completed the seasons of life, experienced the on-going sequence of birth and death, kept the faith, and are no longer terrified by the eventuality of their own death.

Death in the Black community is perceived as a celebration of life, a testament to the fact that a life has been lived, that the earthly journey has been completed. Those who serve as witnesses in the presence of death, extended family, friends, and church members, to affirm the essence of the person's existence are ready to testify to the fact that the deceased has fought the battle, borne the burden, and finished the course; they are ready to understand and say well done. Unlike the Euro-American culture where death is suppressed and the dead and dying are isolated away from public view (Aries, 1980), the passing of life in the Black ethos is an occasion where public festivities are part of the mourning process. In the Black community of New Orleans, the funeral is commemorated with a parade to the cemetery, complete with a jazz band to start the deceased on the next leg of the journey. After the funeral, mourners get together to eat, drink, and talk about happy times with the deceased. The upbeat tone of death in the Black experience has been noted by informal observers. Shortly after the assassination of Robert Kennedy in June of 1968, his sister-in-law, Jacqueline Kennedy Onassis, was talking to Frank Mankiewicz, Kennedy's campaign manager about how the Catholic church was at its best at the time of death. She went on to say "I'll tell you who else understands death are the Black churches. I remember at the funeral of Martin Luther King. I was looking at those faces, and I realized they know death. They see it all the time and they're ready for it."[14]

---

[14]From *Robert Kennedy and His Times*, by Arthur M. Schlesinger, Jr. Copyright © 1978 by Arthur M. Schlesinger Jr. Reprinted by permission of Houghton Mifflin Company.

DISTRUST AND DECEPTION

The experiences of slavery, Jim Crow legislation, de facto and de jure segregation, institutional racism, and the ongoing economic oppression in America have taught Black folks to distrust white folk. There have been too many dreams deferred and promissory notes unpaid by the banks of justice for Blacks to be able to trust the White person's word, laws, and institutions. Above all, the destiny of Afro-Americans cannot be placed in the hands of the Whites. The trust–mistrust issue was at the heart of the great debate during the post-Reconstruction period at the turn of the twentieth century between the accommodationist, Booker T. Washington, and the militant-activist, W. E. B. DuBois. DuBois (1903) was of the opinion that Black folks should not passively surrender their civil, legal and political rights, guaranteed under the equal-protection clause of the Fourteenth Amendment, and depend on the good will of white folks to return these rights when they felt Blacks had demonstrated that they were ready to assume the responsibilities of full citizenship.

The distrust of white folks was a favorite topic at street-corner rallies conducted by the Harlem race of men of a by-gone era, Garveites, curbstone nationalists of all kinds, and members of the Nation of Islam. Drawing on the collective experience of their audiences with white folks, speakers had no trouble producing an uncontested response when they asked rhetorical questions about who was the biggest liar, thief, hypocrite, or gangster in the world. Elijah Muhammad, leader of the Lost Found Nation of Islam in the Wilderness of the North American continent, told it like it was and still is when he accused whites of engaging in a posture of 'tricknology" in their relationships with Black folks (Baldwin, 1963). Stokely Carmichael (1971) repeatedly drew spontaneous affirmation from Black gatherings around the country when he called the white person a liar, hypocrite, and thief, who stole this country from the Indians, lock, stock and barrel, top to bottom, left to right. The Native Americans themselves cosigned Stokely's statement about the theft of the country. In *Bury My Heart at Wounded Knee* (D. Brown, 1970), an aging Indian chief, talks about the broken promises: "The white man made us many promises, more than I can remember, but they never kept but one; they promised to take our land and they took it."[15] When President Lyndon Johnson was accused by the news media of a credibility gap in communicating his policies on the Vietnam War, Stokely came right down in front with his response when he said: "Credibility gap, hell, that honkey is just lying." The Kerner commission (1968), created by the Johnson administration to study the causes of urban unrest, rebellions, and violence in America's Black ghettos, after documenting the history of white racism in America, concluded that Black folks had valid reasons to distrust white institutions, promises, and illusions of significant progress in the elimination of racial oppression.

The Black revolutionaries of the late 1960s, *The Angry Children of Malcolm X* (Lester, 1971), went a step further with the issue of distrust, raising doubts about the substance of Euro-American values. They saw the White culture as decadent, lacking in humanistic concern for others, and they predicted the ultimate death of white civilization with the emergence of a new order of human values based on respect for human dignity. These young activists left us with the question, who would want to integrate with a burning house?

Distrust of the white man, his word, his technology, and his woman is the message expressed in the epic poem "Shine." Shine is the only Black person aboard the supposedly unsinkable Titanic, "the biggest and baddest ship to ever sail the seas"[16] (Simpkins et al., 1971), when it starts on its ill-fated maiden voyage across the Atlantic. Amidst the luxury and splendor of this vast ocean liner, Shine is employed as a laborer in the boiler room, shoveling coal to keep the furnace going. After the ship hits the iceberg and water begins to flood the boiler room, Shine becomes concerned about what's happening and starts to go up on deck to check for himself. The boiler room chief, who has faith in the ship's technology, tells Shine:[17]

[15]D. Brown, *Bury My Heart at Wounded Knee* (New York: Holt, Rinehart and Winston, 1970). Reprinted by permission.

[16]Gary Simpkins, Grace Holt, and Charlesetta Simpkins, *Bridge: A Cross-Cultural Reading Program* (Boston: Houghton Mifflin, 1977). Reprinted by permission.

[17]The version of Shine presented here is taken from the author's memory as he recalls hearing it as an adolescent in the Fillmore district of San Francisco in the 1950s. Other versions of Shine appear in Abrahams (1970), Simpkins (1971), Levine (1977), and Dance (1978).

Shine, Shine, get back below.
I got forty-nine brand new electric pumps to keep that water back.

Shine, who concludes from his direct observation that the ship is sinking, tells the chief:

That may be true and there is little doubt,
But I'll be goddamned if I'll stay here and find out.
I don't like chicken and I don't like ham,
And I don't believe your pumps is worth a damn.

Had he lived in the modern era Shine might have added that "the will of the people is greater than the man's technology." As the epic continues:

When Shine stepped up on the quarter deck,
The symphony orchestra was playing near oh my God to thee;
And the sharks in the water were singing Shine, oh, Shine,
Bring your Black ass to me.

Shine replies to the shark:

I know you outswim the barracuda,
Outsmart every fish in the sea
But you go to be a stroking motherfucker to outswim me.

After Shine dives in the water and demonstrates his aquatic skills, the rich white man, aware of his impending doom, begs Shine to return and save him with pleas of:

Shine, Shine, save poor me,
And I'll make you rich as any Shine can be.

Shine, no doubt recalling the history of broken promises tells the man:

There is money on land and money on sea
But the money on land is better for me.
One thing about you white folks I couldn't understand
You all wouldn't offer me that money when we was all on land.

The alluring, panic-stricken white woman tries to tempt Shine with offers of sex, but Shine will have none of it:

> *The admiral's daughter came out on deck,*
> *She had her drawers wrapped around her head,*
> *And her brassiere in her hand,*
> *She said Shine, oh, Shine, save poor me,*
> *And I'll put this good pussy just where it ought to be.*

Shine tells her:

> *There is pussy on land and pussy on sea,*
> *But the pussy on land is better for me.*
> *If you want to save your white ass,*
> *You better get out here and swim like me.*

The poem ends with:

> *Now, Shine could swim and Shine could float,*
> *Could hit more licks than a motor boat,*
> *Shine swam the Atlantic and Swam the Pacific,*
> *When the Titanic finally sunk*
> *Shine was walkin' round in Alabama, dead drunk.*

In view of the distrust Afro-Americans have developed in their dealings with white folks it should come as no surprise that Black folks have been less than honest, even somewhat deceptive, when it comes to sharing what's really on their minds with white folks as can be seen in the following statements taken from old slave songs and narratives:

> *Got one mind for white folk to see*
> *Nother for what I know is me*
> *He don't know don't know what's on my mind.*[18]

> *You t'inks I'm mistaken, honey! But I know t'ings dat de wite folks wid all dar larnin' nebber fin's out, an' nebber sarches fo' nudder . . .*

---

[18]R. Ames, "Protest and Irony in Negro Folksong." *Social Science*, 14, (1950), pp. 193–213. Reprinted by permission.

No, honey! De good Lawd doan gib ebery-ting to his wite chilluns. He's gib' em de wite skin, an' larnin'. An' he's made 'em rich and free. But de brack folks is his chilluns, too, an' he gibs us de brack skin an' no larnin', an' hab makes us t' work fo' de wite folks. But de good Lawd gib us eyes t' see t'ings dey doan see, an' tells me be patient, 'cause dar's no wite nor brack in hebben. An' de time's commin' when he'll make his brack chilluns free in dis yere worl', an gib' em larnin', and' good homes, an' good times. Ah! honey, I knows, I knows![19]

> "Aunt Aggy"—a Virginia slave in the 1840s.

The use of a common language with culturally different semantics enables Blacks to conceal what they mean from white folks while still maintaining a high level of clarity in their communications. Words, phrases, and statements that are taken to mean one thing when interpreted from a Euro-American frame of reference can mean something entirely different when translated through an Afro-American ethnotropic filter. Familiar gospel tunes sung right under old massa's nose, like "Steal Away to Jesus," "On My Journey Now," and "Dis Train is Bound For Glory," depending on the nature of subtle contextual cues, could be interpreted to mean "I'm getting ready to steal away from here, to start on my journey on a secret train (the underground railroad) bound north to freedom." The implicit determination to stride toward freedom hidden in the multiple meanings of Black gospel music was quickly captured by the nonviolent warriors of the civil rights movement as they adjusted the beat of their marching orders to songs like "Got on My Travelin' Shoes," "We Shall Not Be Moved," "Ain't Gonna Let Nobody Turn Me 'Round," and "Woke Up This Morning With My Mind Set on Freedom."

Linguistic deception can be used as a way of controlling undesirable psychological imagery and devaluative labels propogated by Euro-Americans. A bad nigger in the white folklore is someone who is undesirable. In the cultural semantics of Black folks a bad nigger is a hero, someone who is looked up to for not being afraid to take the risk of standing up to white folks. Black children sometimes confuse their teachers by turning undesirable labels around to indicate admirable personality traits. Teachers apply terms like "clumsy

---

[19]"The Story of my Life," Mary Livermore, (Hartford Conn. 1897) pp. 306–307

lips," suggesting speech deficits, to children who persistently use Black English in the classroom. When the children refer to somebody as having clumsy lips, they mean a brother who can "run it down, talk that talk, and get over" with the power of words (Holt, 1975).

Black teenagers are able to control the flow of conversation in interviews with white authority figures when they shift cultural referents to Black figures of speech and start talking about "holding down corners," "breaking down," "doing the penguin," "fucking with pigs" and "shooting" at fine "foxes."[20] White teenagers trying to copy the language of Black teenagers often get the semantics mixed up; witness the situation where a white girl refers to a big ugly white boy as a "fox."

A classic case of Blacks controlling powerful white folks by a psychology of deception based on the counter tricknology of linguistic nuances, seeming agreement, and some good old-fashioned Sambo-like shuffling, grinnin', and tommin' is Dr. Bledsoe in Ellison's (1952) *Invisible Man*. In a long, rambling tirade excerpted below, Dr. Bledsoe, the president of a small Black southern college, explains the realities of power, control, counter tricknology, and deception in Black-white relationships to an errant protege. The student protege, the unnamed protagonist of Ellison's novel, has endangered the college's existence by exposing a white benefactor to an incestuous Black family and also to a group of mentally deranged but politically astute Black professional lawyers and doctors who were supposed to remain hidden away from the prying eyes of white folks. When the student defends his behavior by explaining that he stopped at these locations because the benefactor "ordered me to," Dr. Bledsoe takes off on him:

> "Ordered you?" he said. "He *ordered* you. Dammit, white folks are always giving orders, it's a habit with them. Why didn't you make an excuse? Couldn't you say they had sickness—smallpox—or picked another cabin? Why that Trueblood shack? My God, boy! You're black and living in the South—did you forget how to lie?"

> "But I was only trying to please him . . . "

[20]Alan Wesson, "The Black Man's Burden: The White Clinician," *The Black Scholar*, 1975 (6), pp. 13–18. Reprinted by permission.

"*Please* him? And here you are a junior in college! Why, the dumbest black bastard in the cotton patch knows that the only way to please a white man is to tell him a lie! What kind of education are you getting around here?

After the protagonist threatens to report him to the trustees, Dr. Bledsoe continues:

"Boy, are *are* a fool," he said. "Your white folks didn't teach you anything and your mother-wit has left you cold. What has happened to you young Negroes? I thought you had caught on to how things are done down here. But you don't even know the difference between the way things are and the way they're supposed to be. "My God," he gasped, "what is the race coming to? Why, boy, you can tell anyone you like—sit down there . . . Sit down, sir, I say!"

"Tell anyone you like," he said. "I don't care. I wouldn't raise my little finger to stop you. Because I don't owe anyone a thing, son. Who, Negroes? Negroes don't control this school or much of anything else—haven't you learned even that? No, sir, they don't control this school, nor white folk either. True they *support* it, but I control it. I's big and black and I say 'Yes, suh' as loudly as any burrhead when its convenient, but I'm still the king down here. I don't care how much it appears otherwise. Power doesn't have to show off. Power is confident, self-assuring, self-starting and self-stopping, self-warming and self-justifying. When you have it, you know it. Let the Negroes snicker and the crackers laugh! Those are the facts, son. The only ones I even pretend to please are *big* white folk, and even those I control more than they control me. This is a power set-up, son, and I'm at the controls. You think about that. When you buck against me, you're bucking against power, rich white folk's power, the nation's power—which means government power!"[21]

CONCLUSIONS

The Black psychological perspective, embodied in the qualities of emotional vitality, realness, resilience, interrelatedness, the value of direct experience, and distrust and deception, determines how

---

[21]Ralph Ellison, *Invisible Man* (New York: Random House, 1952), pp. 107–111. Reprinted by permission.

events are experienced, interpreted, and expressed in the phenomenal field. The failure to acknowledge the existence of a Black psychological perspective or frame of reference has been a source of controversy between Blacks and whites in behavioral science research, education, psychotherapy, child development, and family life. Furthermore, communication between Blacks and whites around complex social realities is problematic because they may not be looking at the issues, such as racial progress, police brutality, and who should control the decision-making apparatus, from a common psychological perspective. In order to move toward resolving the conflicts associated with differences in cultural and psychological perspectives between Blacks and whites, it is essential that the Black perspective be taken into consideration by the policy-making bodies in behavioral science research, social services planning, community mental health, and education.

REFERENCES

ABRAHAMS, ROGER. *Deep Down in the Jungle.* Chicago: Adline Publishing Co., 1970.

AMES, R. "Protest and Irony in Negro Folksong." *Social Science, 14,* (1950), 193–213.

ARIES, PHILIPPE. *The Hour of Our Death.* New York: Knopf, 1980.

BALDWIN, JAMES. *Notes of a Native Son.* New York: Beacon Press, 1955.

———. *The Fire Next Time.* New York: Dial Press, 1963.

———. *Going to Meet the Man.* New York: Dial Press, 1965.

BROWN, CLAUDE. *The Children of Ham.* Briarcliff Manor, N.Y.: Stein & Day, 1973.

BROWN, DEE. *Bury My Heart at Wounded Knee.* New York: Holt, Rinehart and Winston, 1972.

BROWN, H. RAP. *Die Nigger Die.* New York: Dial Press, 1969.

CAMBRIDGE, GODFREY. *Here's Godfrey Cambridge, Ready or Not.* EPIC, Footlight Series.

CARMICHAEL, STOKELY. *Stokely Speaks, Black Power to Pan-Africanism.* New York: Vintage Books, 1971.

CARMICHAEL, STOKELY, and HAMILTON, CHARLES. *Black Power: The Politics of Liberation in America*. New York: Random House, 1967.

CLARK, M., and GOSNELL, M. "The Graying of America." *Newsweek*, February 28, 1977.

CLEAVER, ELDRIDGE. *Soul on Ice*. New York: Dell Pub. Co., 1968.

DANCE, DARYL. *Shuckin' and Jivin': Folklore From Contemporary Black Americans*. Bloomington: Indiana University Press, 1978.

DAVIS, OSSIE. "The Wonderful World of Law and Order," pp. 154–180 in H. Hill, ed., *Anger and Beyond: The Negro Writer in the United States*. New York: Harper & Row, 1968.

DUBOIS, W. E. B. *The Souls of Black Folk*. Chicago: McClurg, 1903.

ELLISON, RALPH. *Invisible Man*. New York: Random House, 1952.

HALBERSTAM, DAVID. *The Best and the Brightest*. New York: Random House, 1971.

HOLT, GRACE. "Metaphor, Black Discourse Style and Cultural Reality," pp. 86–95 in R. L. Williams, ed., *Ebonics, The True Language of Black Folks*. St. Louis: Institute of Black Studies, 1975.

HUGHES, LANGSTON. *Simple Speaks His Mind*. New York: Simon & Schuster, 1950.

———. *Simple Takes a Wife*. New York: Simon & Schuster, 1953.

———. "Mother to Son," in *Selected Poems* by Langston Hughes. New York: Knopf, 1954.

———. *Simple Takes a Claim*. New York: Holt, Rinehart & Rinehart, 1957.

JACKSON, MAHALIA. "How I Got Over" from the album, *Mahalia Jackson Sings the Best-Loved Hymns of Dr. Martin Luther King, Jr.* New York: Columbia Records, 1968.

JEFFERS, LANCE. "Afro-American Literature, The Conscience of Man," *The Black Scholar*, January 1971, pp. 47–53.

JONES, LEROI. *Blues People: Negro Music in White America*. New York: Morrow, 1963.

KING, MARTIN LUTHER, JR. "I have a Dream," speech delivered at the March on Washington, August 1963. pp. 346–351 in A. Meier, E. Rudwick, and F. L. Broderick, eds., *Black Protest Thought in the Twentieth Century* (2nd ed.). New York: Bobbs-Merrill, 1971.

KERNER, OTTO (Chairman). *Report of the National Commission on Civil Disorders: U.S. Riot Commission Report.* New York: Bantam Books, 1968.

KNIGHT, GLADYS. "I've Got to Use My Imagination," from the album, *Imagination.* New York: Budda Records, 1973.

LESTER, JULIUS. "The Angry Children of Malcolm X," in Thomas Fraizer, ed., *Afro-American History Primary Sources.* New York: Harcourt Brace Jovanovich, 1971.

LEVINE, LAWRENCE. *Black Culture and Black Consciousness: Afro-American Folk Thought from Slavery to Freedom.* New York: Oxford University Press, 1977.

LEWIS, DAVID. *King, A Critical Biography.* Baltimore: Penguin, 1971.

LIVERMORE, MARY. *The Story of My Life.* Hartford, Conn.: 1897.

LOMAX, LEWIS. "The American Negro's New Comedy Act," *Harper,* June 1961, pp. 41–46.

MALCOLM X. *The Autobiography of Malcolm X.* New York: Grove Press, 1965.

NEAL, LARRY. "The Ethos of the Blues." *The Black Scholar,* Summer 1972, pp. 42–48.

NOBLES, WADE. "Black People in White Insanity: An Issue for Community Mental Health," *Journal of Afro-American Issues,* no. *4,* 1 (Winter 1976) 21–27.

PRYOR, RICHARD. "Mudbone," from the album *Richard Pryor, Is It Something I Said?* New York: Reprise Records, 1975.

———. *Richard Pryor's Greatest Hits.* New York: Warner Brothers Records, 1977.

REDMOND, EUGENE. "The Black American Epic: Its Roots, Its Writers," *The Black Scholar,* January 1971, pp. 15–22.

SCHLESINGER, ARTHUR J. *Robert Kennedy and His Times.* Boston: Houghton Mifflin, 1978.

SIMPKINS, GARY; HOLT, GRACE; AND SIMPKINS, CHARLESETTA. *Bridge, A Cross-Cultural Reading Program.* Boston: Houghton Mifflin, 1977.

SMITH, ERNIE. "Evolution and Continuing Presence of the Oral Tradition in Black America." Doctoral Dissertation submitted to the University of California, Irvine, Fall 1974.

SMITHERMAN, GENEVA. *Talkin and Testifyin.* Boston: Houghton Mifflin, 1977.

SPILLERS, HORTENSE. "Martin Luther King and the Style of the Black Sermon," *The Black Scholar,* September 1971, 14–27.

WARREN, ROBERT P. *Who Speaks For the Negro?* New York: Random House, Inc., 1965.

WESSON, ALAN. "The Black Man's Burden: The White Clinician," *The Black Scholar, 6,* (1975) 13–18.

WITHERS, BILL. "Grandma's Hands," from the album, *Bill Withers Live at Carnegie Hall.* Hollywood: Sussex Records, 1971.

WRIGHT, RICHARD. *Black Boy.* New York: Harper & Row, 1945.

———. *American Hunger.* New York: Harper & Row, 1977.

CHAPTER THREE

PSYCHOSOCIAL DYNAMICS OF BLACK FAMILY LIFE

INTRODUCTION

The emerging view of Black family life is that its underlying genotype, its basic structure, consists of an extended family group made up of a number of legally related and nonlegally related adults and children who come together within a mutually supportive social, psychological, and economic network to deal conjointly with the responsibilities of living (Stack, 1974). This pattern of family life with its emphasis on mutual solidarity, cooperation, and interdependence originated in Africa and has persisted despite its going through several cycles of formation, breakup, and reformulation brought about by slavery, a century of migration out of the rural South, and restrictive welfare codes (Nobles, 1978). During the periods of breakup and reformulation the extended family may take on a different surface or phenotypical appearance; however, if the Black family is observed across sufficient time and geographical space, its basic extended structure will reappear (Gutman, 1976).

THE DEFICIT-DEFICIENCY MODEL

The view of the core structure of the Black family as an extended family grouping is not shared by all observers. The traditional view of the Black family, which has evolved from the works of Frazier

(1939), Elkins (1968), Moynihan (1965), and Rainwater (1970), is one of a disorganized, single-parent, subnuclear, female-dominated social system. This is essentially the deficit-deficiency model of Black family life. The deficit-deficiency model begins with the historical assumption that there was no carry-over from Africa to America of any sophisticated African-based form of family life and communal living. Viable patterns of family life either did not exist because Africans were incapable of creating them, or they were destroyed beginning with slavery and the separation of biological parents and children, forced breeding, the master's sexual exploitation of Black women, and the accumulative effects of three hundred years of economic and social discrimination. As a result of this background of servitude, deprivation, second-class citizenship, and chronic unemployment, Black adults have not been able to develop marketable skills, self-sufficiency, future orientation, and planning and decision-making competencies, instrumental behaviors thought to be necessary for sustaining a successful two-parent nuclear family while guiding the children through the socialization process.

In a society that placed a premium on decisive male leadership in the family, the Black male was portrayed as lacking the masculine sex role behaviors characterized by logical thinking, willingness to take responsibility for others, assertiveness, managerial skills, achievement orientation, and occupational mastery. The Black male in essence had been psychologically castrated and rendered ineffective by forces beyond his control. He is absent within the family circle and unable to provide leadership and command respect when he is present. After generations of being unable to achieve the ideal male role in the family and in American society, the Black male is likely to be inclined to compensate for his failure by pursuing roles such as the pimp, player, hustler, and sweet daddy, which are in conflict with the norms of the larger society. The appearance of these roles in male behavior in the Black community, rather than being interpreted as a form of social protest, reinforces the majority culture stereotypes of Black males as irresponsible, lazy, shiftless, and sociopathic.

The Black woman does not fare much better in terms of how she is portrayed in the deficit-deficiency model of Black family life. She is regarded as the head of the household, a matriarch who initially received her power because the society was unwilling to permit the Black male to assume the legal, economic, and social positions necessary to become a dominant force within the family and community life. Having achieved this power by default, the Black female is unwilling to share it. Her unwillingness to share her power persists even when the Black male is present and willing to assume responsibility in the family circle, since she is not confident of the male's ability to follow through on his commitments. Confrontation over decision making and family direction is usually not necessary because the Black male is either not present in the household on any ongoing basis or is regarded as ineffective by the female when he is present.

The impact of the matriarchial family on the sex-role development of the children in relationship to the dominant social system, which has a precedent for clearly distinguishing between acceptable male and female social roles, is considered to be devastating. The Black male child has no adequate father figure to emulate in acquiring the conventional masculine instrumental behaviors typified by responsibility taking, resourcefulness, independence, occupational preparation, and cool-headed, logical decision making. To make matters worse, the mother may ventilate her anger and disappointment with the father for not being able to fulfill his role as a provider on the male child by expressing an attitude that men are no good, irresponsible, and only interested in conquering women sexually. When trying to discourage behavior that she considers undesirable, the mother is likely to compare the child to his father by telling him that he is going to turn out to be a no-count man, just like his father. The effect of an absent role model, coupled with the negative image of masculinity that is being projected, prevents the male child from acquiring the confidence he needs to resolve successfully the issues associated with his identity and psychosexual development as he evolves through adolescence and early adulthood. The final outcome of this female-dominated socialization process is the creation of still another generation of Black males who will be unable to build the internal security and social role skills necessary to become heads of households, interact productively in relationships with women, and serve as sound role models for their own children.

The Black female child, on the other hand, is constantly exposed to a cadre of women in authority and decision-making roles within the family—not only her own mother, but a community of women made up of aunties, grandmothers, cousins, and other women neighbors who occupy the same positions in their families. Presented with this abundance of feminine role models without the balancing input from adult males in fatherlike roles, the Black female child is vulnerable to developing an exaggerated notion of her own role as a future adult and parent. She has no real idea of what male–female teamwork is all about, since she has had very little, if any, exposure to decision-making models where the male is part of the process. To further complicate matters, she has also heard her mother and other adult females bad-mouth Black males for their inability to take care of business. She has been admonished to learn to take care of herself and not to become dependent on some no-count man who would be unable to fulfill his responsibilities. In short, she has been told to "keep her pants up and her dress down," lest she fall victim to a situation where she will have a flock of children with no father to assist her in the child-rearing process.

When the offspring of these matriarchial families meet in the next generation as adults, it is difficult to conceive of how they could develop a mutually satisfying relationship. The male is confused, doesn't know who he is, and lacks the emotional maturity required for the ongoing responsibilities of family living. The Black female has an exaggerated sense of her own worth, doesn't have much confidence in the male's ability to meet his obligations over a prolonged period of time, and has very little preparation for the give-and-take of male–female relationships. These kinds of sisters have been known to sell their men "woof tickets" with statements to the effect of "I was working and taking care of myself when I met you, I'm working and taking care of myself now, and I'll be working and taking care of myself when I leave you." Putting two people like these, who have been reared in matriarchial families, together in a conjugal union or marriage of their own would seem to represent the beginnings of another vicious, destructive, deficit-deficiency cycle with the "web and tangle of pathology" recreating itself.

The proponents of the pathology-oriented, matriarchial family model did not consider the possibility that a single-parent Black mother could serve as an adequate role model for the children of both sexes. The notion that the mother could reflect a balance of the traditional male and female roles, with respect to mental toughness and emotional tenderness, was largely ignored because of the rigid classification of psychosexual roles in American society. In the Black community, however, the categorization of social role behaviors based on gender is not as inflexible. It is conceivable that a Black mother could project a combination of assertive and nurturant behaviors in the process of rearing children of both sexes as nonsexist adults.

With the reality of accelerating divorce rates, in recent years the single-parent family headed by a woman has become a social reality in Euro-America. This reality has been accompanied by an attempt on the part of social scientists to legitimate family structures that represent alternatives to the nuclear family while reconceptualizing the social roles of males and females with less emphasis on exclusive behaviors. The concept of androgyny has been introduced to cover the vast pool of human personality traits that can be developed by either sex (Rogers, 1978). A well-balanced person reflects a combination of both instrumental and expressive traits. The latter include feeling-oriented behaviors formerly considered feminine, such as tenderness, caring, and affection. Thus, it is conceptually possible for a white, single androgynous female parent to rear psychologically healthy, emotionally integrated children. It is intersting how the sociology of the times makes available to white Americans psychological concepts designed to legitimatize changes in the family, in child-rearing patterns, and in relationships between the sexes. Yet, these same behaviors when first expressed by Afro-Americans were considered as pathological.

THE EXTENDED FAMILY MODEL

The extended family, in contrast to the single-parent subnuclear family, consists of a related and quasi-related group of adults, including aunts, uncles, parents, cousins, grandparents, boyfriends, and girl friends linked together in a kinship or kinlike network. They form a cooperative interface with each other in confronting the concerns of living and rearing the children. This model of family life, which seems able to capture not only the strength, vitality, resilience, and continuity of the Black family, but also the essence of Black values, folkways, and life styles, begins with a different set of assumptions about the development and evolution of Black family life in America.

The Black extended family is seen as an outgrowth of African patterns of family and community life that survived in America. The Africans carried with them through the Mid-Atlantic passage and sale to the initial slave owners a well-developed pattern of kinship, exogamous mating, and communal values, emphasizing collective survival, mutual aid, cooperation, mutual solidarity, interdependence, and responsibility for others (Nobles, 1974; Blassingame, 1972). These values became the basis for the Black extended family in America. They were retained because they were familiar and they allowed the slaves to have some power over destiny by enabling them to develop their own styles for family interaction. A consciousness of closeness to others, belongingness, and togetherness protected the slave from being psychologically destroyed by feelings of despair and alienation and the extended family provided a vehicle to pass the heritage on to the children (Fredrickson, 1976; Gutman, 1976). Slaves in essence created their own communal family space, regardless of whether the master was paternalistic or conducted a Nazilike concentration camp.

To understand the cultural continuity, it is necessary to depart from the traditional hypothesis that slave masters and their descendants exercised total psychological and social control over the development of Black family life and community institutions. The slaves were much more than empty psychological tablets on which the master imprinted an identity. These early Blacks were able to find ways of creating psychological space and implementing African cultural forms that whites were unaware of and did not understand. Once in the New World the African recreated a sense of tribal community within the plantation milieu through a series of extended kin and kinlike family networks that carried on the cultural values of responsibility for others, mutual aid and collective survival. First- and second-generation American slaves who were separated from biological kin by continued activity at the auction block and newly arriving slaves who were sold to different plantations were

incorporated into the extended family structures of existing plantations. It was not essential for the survival of African conceptions of
family life that biological or legal kinship ties be maintained. When a
people share a philosophy of interdependence and collective survival, persons who are not biologically or legally related can become
interwoven into newly created and existing kinlike networks. Cultural patterns once established seem to endure, especially if they
work. The extended family survived because it provided Afro-
Americans a support system within the context of a shared frame of
reference. Along with other African customs and beliefs, an African
family identity was passed along to the children as the link between
generations through the oral tradition.

Once the philosophy of collective survival and interdependence was set into place as the foundation for community living, the
extended family evolved through a series of cycles of formation,
breakup, and reformation as the slaves who were without the re-
course to legal rights to protect kinship structures and conjugal
unions were transferred from place to place. Much later, with the
beginnings of the Industrial Revolution after the Civil War, the
pattern of Black family life based on combinations of kinship and
kinlike networks continued, despite the emergence of the nuclear
family among Euro-Americans. The growth of the individual nuclear family in Euro-America seemed to correspond with the competitive and individualistic values of the market place. The cycles of
formation, breakup, and reformation of the extended family continued as Blacks migrated farther north and west towards the cities
at the turn of the century during the pre and post periods of the two
world wars and into the modern age.

According to Gutman (1976), who in his extensive studies of
the Black family used vital statistics of births, deaths, and conjugal
unions kept in plantation ledgers, census bureau statistics, and regional and local population records, the true structure of the Black
family only emerges when the Black family is observed over a period
of at least two or three generations. It seems to go through four
identifiable stages. The phenotypical structure may appear to be
different at selected times during the transition periods, but the
underlying genotype is one that involves a sense of communalism,
interdependence, collective survival, and mutual aid.

The first stage, beginning in Africa or with a stable plantation population, involves an extended family composed of biologically related kin who are socially connected with similar groups to form a community. In the second stage the biological kin network becomes scattered as a result of trades or later by succesive migrations. During the third stage the remaining individual and newly arriving Blacks come together in a combination of new kinship and kinlike structures. During this period the extended family is being rebuilt through new conjugal unions, marriages between young people, and the arrival of some folks who were members of the original family. In the fourth stage the extended family is completely visible again.

The Black extended family, with its grandparents, biological parents, conjugal partners, aunts, uncles, cousins, older siblings, boyfriends, girl friends and quasi-kin, is an intergenerational group. The members of this three-generation family do not necessarily reside in the same household. Individual households are part of a sociofamilial network that functions like a minicommunity. The members band together to share information, resources, and communal concern (Stack, 1974). There is no central authority, matriarchial or patriarchial. Decisions are made on an equalitarian model with input and outcomes determined by who is available at a given time, who has expertise with reference to a given problem, and one's prior experience and track record in decision making. This is likely to give some edge to the tribal elders. They are looked up to within the extended family network as resource people and advisors because they have the life experience that is highly valued in the Black community. As in the past, the family is held together over time and across geographical space by a shared experience frame and a common set of values involving interdependence, mutual aid, resilience, communalism, and collective responsibility (Nobles, 1978). These values transcend sex roles and allow both men and women to participate in and contribute to the management of economic resources, child rearing, community activism, and other issues of family life without being categorically restricted on the basis of gender. The fluid distinction between social sex roles offers both men and women in the Black family network the opportunity to emerge as decision makers, influence molders, and household managers.

It could be argued that the Black extended family exists and persists primarily because Black people face the common fate of oppressive economic and social conditions, that it exists out of necessity as a way of surviving in an oppressive class system. Politically and economically oppressed people have historically banded together for survival, whether it be in internment camps, labor unions, or women's movements. It would follow from this argument that the Black extended family would disappear as Black people moved up the socioeconomic ladder. Yet the extended family does not appear to be disappearing with rising economic fortunes. MacAdoo's (1979) work with upwardly mobile middle and upper-middle class Black families suggest that not only does the extended family model persist when Blacks move up the socioeconomic ladder but the Afro-American values of mutual aid, interdependence, and interconnectedness also remain as the guiding ethos of family existence.

Being part of a close-knit extended family group is a vital part of Afro-American life. Wherever Blacks appear in numbers of two or more, whether it be on predominately white college campuses, professional baseball teams, fraternal groups, street corners, storefront churches, automobile factories, or professional conferences, they soon seem to form a quasi-family network, share information and resources, get together, git down, rap, and party. White folks don't know what to make of this. The idea of sharing, closeness, and interdependence expressed in sociofamilial groups is so deeply ingrained in the fabric of the Afro-American ethos that it is not likely to give way to the nuclear family with its stress on isolation, competition, and independence. If anything, the traditional nuclear family may be moving toward becoming more like the Afro-American extended family.

To the extent that the extended family model represents a more accurate way of categorizing the Black family and capturing its strengths, the question arises as to why generations of the Black ghetto's Euro-American occupation army represented by sociologists, their graduate students, census takers, welfare workers, law-enforcement personnel, and bill collectors could only find broken, disorganized, single-parent, female-dominated families. The answer to this question involves several complex, interrelated reasons.

First, white observers may have been guided by a constricted cultural frame of reference where the only viable form of family life consisted of a two-parent family contained within the boundaries of a single household. When they didn't find this single household nuclear family operating in the Black community, their constricted model prevented them from being able to access correctly the differences they observed. They mistakenly labeled differences as deviant, therefore pathological.

Second, Black folks themselves have been known to be deceptive about the membership of their families when being questioned by authorities representing the white establishment whom they mistrust, such as law-enforcement personnel, bill collectors, and welfare workers. Given the restrictive nature of the welfare system, it is not hard to imagine why a Black woman would not be truthful to a public assistance worker about the nature of her conjugal relationships, regardless of whether they involve a legal husband, boyfriend, sweet daddy, or transient male friend. Carol Stack (1974) contends that the welfare system as it was traditionally structured worked against the emergence of stable conjugal unions within the extended family.

Third, the very nature of white institutions works against the Black extended family as it attempts to fulfill its collective responsibilities and functions within the context of Afro-American values (Nobles, 1978). Wade Nobles, a nationally recognized expert on the Black family, tells a story about moving his nephew, a high school student, from the boy's mother's residence in Louisiana to his household in Berkeley, California. There were no major psychosocial adjustment problems associated with the nephew's making the transition from the Louisiana branch of the Nobles extended family to the Berkeley, California, branch. The problem came about when Dr. Nobles attempted to explain to the Internal Revenue Service how he came by an adolescent dependent in the space of one year with no legal papers to back him up. If Professor Nobles, who holds a Ph.D. from Stanford University, had difficulty explaining the composition of his extended family with the addition of this adolescent nephew, try to imagine what low-income Black aunties or grandmothers go through when they are trying to get aid for dependent children residing in their household who are not their biological or legal offspring, or for that matter what Black college freshmen go through trying to explain the income of their multiple extended-family parents divided by the number of dependent cousins, siblings, nieces, nephews, and fictional kin to college financial aid officers.

Finally, the true nature of the Black family may be clouded by confusing an observation of a phenotype at any given moment with the underlying or basic genotype as the Black family goes through periods of emergence and reemergence. A Black family moving through the rural to urban transition or following jobs from one urban environment to another may at any given observational point, while it is reforming by building new groupings and reestablishing old networks, appear to be a single-parent home, a nuclear family, or a partially developed extended family. All three models can coexist within the core structure and dynamics of the extended family.

The Black child growing up in the extended family is exposed to a variety of role models covering a wide age span whose social behaviors are not completely regulated by conventional sex roles. This offers the children a greater opportunity to incorporate a balanced pattern of expressive and instrumental behaviors. Since parents may not be equally effective as role models at every stage of the child's development, the presence of a range of role models allows the children a series of options at any stage of their development in terms of adults they might seek out for guidance. Other issues concerning the psychosocial development of Black children will be discussed at greater length in Chapter Four.

THE EXTENDED FAMILY
AND ADULT DEVELOPMENTAL TASKS

The three-generation Black extended family offers late adolescents, young adults, and young middle adults the opportunity to continue their growth and development in a supportive environment where they can utilize older adults as counselors and role models. Black parents can evolve their parenting skills while being in direct contact with their own parents and parent surrogates. There are a series of predictable adult crises, typified by financial setbacks, the breakup of conjugal unions, illness, death of loved ones, the realization that one is not going to live forever, and an awareness of the reality that all the major life goals laid out in late adolescence are not going to be accomplished (Sheehy, 1977). In addition to these "passages" or critical periods, the Black adult has to cope with the social and economic obstacles created by the residual effects of racism in America throughout the life cycle. Internalizing a comprehensive understanding of the Afro-American ethos will help the adult to develop the coping skills and internal strength necessary to continue growing and actualizing throughout the life cycle.

The comprehensive mastery and appreciation of the Black ethos is the major developmental task of Black adulthood. As the person gains a more mature awareness of the Black psychological perspective, he or she will be able to experience sorrow without being overwhelmed by a sense of despair and futility; he or she will learn how to experience the joy and pain of loving others, how to open oneself up to the power of renewal, how to discover one's capacity to keep on keepin' on, how to gain strength from being part of something larger than oneself, part of a vital life force that has continued to emerge despite the harshness of oppression, how to avoid seeking personal affirmation from the oppressor, and how to deal with "the man's" tricknology. The Black extended family is the vehicle through which this consciousness is transmitted and developed.

The Black aged are generally not isolated in distant retirement communities or confined to the loneliness of nursing homes. They are functional members of the extended family circle who experience the intimacy of close relationships, contribute valuable insights into the decision-making process, and participate in the excitement and disappointment of living as life unfolds for the generations behind them. Their presence in the extended family provides a certain steadiness, a calming effect on younger adults and young middle-aged adults as they are moving through the critical periods of adult development. As we noted in Chapter Two, "you don't git to be old bein' no fool." The Black elderly, like the *griots* in Africa, are the living reservoirs of the Afro-American heritage contained in the oral tradition. They have been down the line, been through the process of tragedy and renewal, built up a wealth of life experiences, and know how to cope with life. The elderly teach the collective ethos by example and through a host of proverbs, stories, and anecdotes.

Black grandparents are very much involved in the activities of the Black community and were active participants in the marches, demonstrations, and boycotts of the civil rights movement. During the Montgomery, Alabama, bus boycotts in 1955 a Black grandmother told a reporter she was walking to her job as a housemaid every day so that her grandchildren could someday ride on the front of the bus.

The three-generation family allows its members to experience life in retrospect and prospect in a mutually supportive atmosphere. The elderly can look back and see the life cycle being re-created. They can live out their twilight years with dignity in an atmosphere of caring and belongingness, rather than feeling useless, abandoned, helpless, and forgotten. This sense of belongingness, caring, and active involvement mitigates against the fear of death. Children can look ahead and see the whole life cycle unfold in front of them in a natural sequence of events. They are not estranged from the elderly like their white suburban counterparts. Many white children who have never had any day-to-day experience with older people see them as mean, cranky old monsters. Black children learn to appreciate and admire people their grandparents' age through involvement in ongoing relationships with them. With the passing of the elderly, Black youth begin to learn how to cope with the experience of death and mourning.

THE EXTENDED FAMILY AND THE BLACK CHURCH

The Black church consists of a group of extended family networks united together under a common spiritual and social bond. The Black church with its ministers, deacons, elders, brothers, sisters, and children revolves around the familial values of mutual aid, interdependence, sharing, and collective solidarity. Ministers such as Adam Clayton Powell (1945) and Martin Luther King, Jr., (1958) understood the potential force of the Black church as an agent for social change based on a philosophy of collective mass action. Utilizing the extended family networks connected to the Black church as a base, they organized the collective force of the Black community. Through the power of the word they were able to activate within the Black commmunity a consciousness that the possibility of social change was a reality. King (1963) prophesied the change in his famous "March on Washington" speech when he told the audience to "Go back to Mississippi, go back to Alabama, go back to South Carolina, go back to Louisiana, go back to the slums and the ghettos of our northern cities knowing that somehow this situation can and will be changed."[1] Black people who became involved in the movement as activists and fellow travelers recognized that the force of collective action based on a consciousness of brotherhood and a search for equal justice extended far beyond the finite power of self. The exprience of solidarity and support that existed within this collective effort for social change generated a sense of renewal and revitalization in many of the participants.

ISSUES IN MALE–FEMALE RELATIONSHIPS

The ideal male–female relationship within extended family networks and in the Black commmunity at large would be one characterized by the Afro-American values of interdependence, cooperation, and mutual respect, without a fixed classification of household, economic, and social responsibilities based on sex. Male–female relationships that are built on a bond of sharing, nurturance, tenderness, and appreciation have the strong psychological foundation necessary to cope with the social and economic stresses that usually confront Black couples living in a country dominated by Euro-Americans.

---

[1]From "I Have a Dream" by Martin Luther King, Jr. Copyright © 1963 by Martin Luther King, Jr. Reprinted by permission of Joan Daves.

Black males and females have perpetually shown a special interest, delight, attractiveness, and rapture towards members of the opposite sex. Black blues singers and poets have tried to capture the fascination, sensuousness, and euphoria of this mutual attractiveness. James Baldwin (1963) speaks of the "incredibly moving exuberance" Big Bill Broonzy expresses when he sings about feeling so good while on his way to meet his lady at the train station. Aretha Franklin (1969) captures the power of sensuality to remedy minor physical body aches and pains in a song that clearly shows her preference for "Dr. Feelgood" over pain killers, mood elevators, and antidepressants. The nineteenth-century Black poet, Paul Laurence Dunbar (1968) writes in a "Negro Love Song" of the sheer delight he experiences in walking his lady home, holding her hand, and putting his arm around her waist:

> *"Seen my lady home las' night,*
> *Jump back, honey, jump back.*
> *"Hel huh han' an sque'z it tight,*
> *Jump back, honey, jump back.*
> *Hyeahd huh sigh a little sigh,*
> *Seen a light gleam f'om huh eye,*
> *An' a smile go flitten by—*
> *Jump back, honey, jump back.*
>
> *Hyeahd de win' blow thoo de pine,*
> *Jump back, honey, jump back.*
> *Mocking bird was singing fine,*
> *Jump back honey,*
> *An my heart was beatin' so,*
> *When I reached my lady's do',*
> *Dat I couldn't ba' to go—*
> *Jump back, honey, jump back.*
>
> *Put my ahm aroun' huh wais'*
> *Jump back, honey, jump back.*
> *Raised huh lips and took a tase,*
> *Jump back, honey, jump back.*
> *Love me, honey, love me true?*
> *Love me well ez I love you?*
> *And she answe'd "'cose I do'"*
> *Jump back, honey, jump back.*[2]

[2]Paul Laurence Dunbar, *The Complete Poems of Paul Laurence Dunbar* (New York: Dodd, Mead and Co., Inc.) Reprinted by permission.

The contemporary Black poet Margaret Walker (1942) speaks of the capacity of "Poppa Chicken," a sweet daddy, who rhapsodizes and enchants the sisters by his very presence:

> *"Poppa was a sugah daddy*
> *Pimping in his prime;*
> *All the gals for miles around*
> *Walked to Pappa's time.*
>
> *Poppa's face was long and black;*
> *Pappa's grin was broad.*
> *When Poppa Chicken walked the streets*
> *The gals cried lawdy! lawd!*
>
> *Poppa smoked his long cigars—*
> *Special Poppa brands—*
> *Rocks all glis'ning in his tie;*
> *On his long Black hands . . ."[3]*

Black people understand, however, that male–female relationships cannot be maintained in the dream world of perpetual bliss and eternal paradise. In real-world romantic encounters dues have to be paid. Soul folks understand what Lou Rawls means when he sings about love having its painful moments. Prior to the 1960s, before white singers tried to copy the earthiness of the Black blues singers, their love songs seemed to indicate that eternal paradise was possible. There was a tendency to deny the painful possibilities associated with romance—a whitewash, so to speak (Levine, 1977). Black blues singers such as Ma Rainy, Billie Holiday, and Bessie Smith have never denied the reality of a certain amount of pain, sorrow, and loneliness as part of the love relationship (Southern, 1971). Love, like life, has moments of joy and moments of pain. Those who want to sustain productive, intimate relationships with members of the opposite sex must be willing to understand that disappointment is part of the process. The prospect of pain, hardship, rejection, unrequited love, and being left alone in a big room with an empty bed does not seem to discourage the desire of Black folks to seek out heterosexual intimacy. The fascination, intrigue, and obsession with

[3]Margaret Walker, *For My People* (New Haven: Yale University Press, 1942). Reprinted by permission of Margaret Walker Alexander.

members of the opposite sex is an ongoing phenomenon with each successive generation of Black males and females. Brothers at every echelon in American life respond when a super fine sister walks by and are likely to inquire as to where she is going with her bad self; the sisters dig it, even when they pretend they aren't interested (Smitherman, 1977).

The earlier comment, however, about love being a hurtin' thing is a very apropos depiction of the status of affairs in male–female relationships in contemporary Afro-America. One of the major subjects of discussion in places where Blacks congregate in mixed and single groups—barber shops, beauty shops, churches, college dorms, conferences, and the perennial street corner—is what is happening and not happening in male–female relationships, and how the members of the opposite sex are misbehaving and not acting right. Conflicts, disappointments, faulty expectations, and remedies for success in male–female relationships have been the topics of a series of recent books, plays, and periodicals.

Michele Wallace (1979) in her book *Black Males and the Myth of the Super Woman* discusses faulty expectations on both sides. Black poet Ntozake Shange (1977) discusses the trials and tribulations of Black women in their encounters with men in her award-winning Broadway play, *For Colored Girls Who Have Considered Suicide When the Rainbow is Enuf* and Black psychologist-sociologist Nathan Hare and his wife Julia have started a bimonthly magazine entitled *Black Male–Female Relationships* to provide a forum for informative articles and discussion topics.

In analyzing this seemingly endless series of dialogues, debates, and commentary about what's happening in Black male–female relationships, one can detect at least four unproductive relationship styles—unproductive in the sense that the relationships are not built on values that result in mutually satisfying and actualizing experiences for both members of the relationship.

The first two counterproductive relationship styles tend to be characteristic of upwardly mobile brothers and sisters who are trying to put together relationships based on Euro-American life styles and customs. In the first of these Euro-American–oriented relationship styles, Blacks try to develop a relationship style based on the rigid separation of masculine and feminine roles found in the traditional nuclear family. The male perceives himself as, or is expected to be, family leader, major decision maker, and primary breadwinner. As the dominant force in the relationship, he does not expect his decisions to be questioned, and he feels that certain privileges accrue to him because he is a man. The woman is expected to be a follower, not to question the authority of the male, and to take the primary responsibility for rearing the children and managing the household. When she proves to be an effective decision maker, earns as much or more money than her husband, and wants to be recognized as an equal, the whole relationship is thrown off balance. Furthermore, the male may not be able to carry out his macho John Wayne image of being totally self-reliant and emotionally contained in every crisis situation. Even John Wayne found that there were some real-life situations he could not overcome. The couple may not realize until it is too late that the relationship is set up on psychologically repressive, competitive, sexist values, values that Euro-Americans are in the process of abandoning. A relationship based on rigidly defined sex roles prevents men and women from being able to exercise creative choices in deciding what they want from the relationship, what identities they are trying to fashion for themselves, and how they can come together on mutually satisfying terms.

The second counterproductive relationship style seems to be a by-product of Black folks trying to emulate the "me" generation. The psychology of the late 1960s and 1970s brought with it a considerable focus on growth, exploration, and gratification of the self. While the self-actualists who lead the human potential movement may not have intended it, a kind of narcissistic love of self (Lasch, 1979), me first, I am the "great god-damn" syndrome emerged. Some first-generation Black professionals, products of extended families who underwent considerable hardship and sacrifice to help them complete their educations, fall into this syndrome. They seem obsessed with thoughts about their own importance, how they were the first Black in their family to attend a prestigious white university, the first to receive a professional degree, the first of their peer group to receive a high-status job with a top one-hundred firm or an appointment to a highly influential political office, and so on. They have become so caught up in their own advancement and development that they can only look at a male–female relationship in terms of what it can do to satisfy their own needs, career timetables, and inflated self-images. Excessive narcissism goes counter to the grain of any productive relationship, which should have as its foundation mutual satisfaction, reciprocity, and interdependence. Such self-inflated brothers and sisters often end up very much alone and isolated from close, intimate ongoing relationships, not only from members of the opposite sex, but from members of their own sex as well. They feel that others who fail to appreciate them are either envious or don't understand the importance of their goals. What these self-centered people fail to understand is that other brothers and sisters get tired of having to hear about how brilliant they are, how fine they are and how important they are. They would much rather set up a relationship with someone who is real, who can be open, and who is able to reach out and give to others as opposed to always taking.

The third syndrome appears to be an outcome of oppressive economic conditions, compounded by the dehumanizing racism of the welfare system. Not only has it been difficult for Black males as a group to develop marketable skills, but they have not been allowed a wide range of options to utilize whatever skills they were able to develop. In addition, until the late 1960s the welfare system made it difficult for the male to reside in the household with his family if the family was drawing public assistance. Exclusion from the home after experiencing a long series of economic setbacks is devastating to a man's pride. Some Black women who didn't fully understand the cumulative nature of economic and social forces working against the Black male may have come to the conclusion that they did not need the male economically or psychologically. They could survive better, economically speaking, without the males, since it was then easier to receive welfare benefits for dependent children. This type of thinking is not representative of the majority of low-income Black women. Nonetheless, it does represent a potential source of conflict in male–female relationships among low-income Blacks.

The final unproductive pattern of Black male-female relationships is represented by brothers and sisters—especially brothers—running a game on each other. This syndrome is characterized by blatant dishonesty and exploitation. Black folks become so caught up in the deceptive nature of the street logic they employ in running games on "the man" that they no longer make distinctions between running games on "the man" and the use of a pimping, hustling mentality in male–female relationships. In the gaming syndrome Blackness can be distorted and used as a cover for exploitation. Back in the days when the Black revolution was the "in" thing in the streets and on college campuses, especially with Black students on predominantly white campuses and among Blacks who were rediscovering Blackness, some of the brothers tried to use the Black liberation struggle as a cover to manipulate sisters into giving them some "pussy for the open revolution."

To further complicate matters, there are certain facts about population statistics that must be taken into consideration in any discussion of male–female relationships in the Black community. Black females clearly outnumber Black males from birth throughout the life cycle. In the twenty-four to forty-four-year-old age group, according to 1977 census data cited by Weathers (1979), there are 732,000 more Black females than males. When these raw figures are combined with the number of brothers who are unavailable for prolonged periods because they are involved with white girls, in the military service, in jail, or on drugs or who have dropped out from sheer mental and physical exhaustion, the statistical discrepancy becomes even more alarming.

Black psychologists, guided by their understanding of the social forces that impact on human relationships, have been conducting a series of workshops, seminars, and interpersonal encounter groups designed to help Black males and females sort out the confusion, conflicting expectations, and faulty communication that prevent the development of more actualizing relationships (Weathers, 1979). To the extent that male–female relationships can be built on the Afro-American values of genuineness, appreciation, likability, and interdependence, a variety of workable relationships and combinations of relationships are possible: serial monogamy and the sharing of available partners, in addition to the traditional one-on-one, long-term relationship. The key element in viable male–female relationships is honesty, clarity of expectations, and a mutual understanding of the social forces that impinge on Black folks in America.

CONCLUSION

The deficit-deficiency model of Black family life in America represents a case where viewing Black family life through the inappropriate lens of the nuclear family contributed significantly to the perception of pathology and deviance. The emergence of the extended family model as a way of conceptualizing the Black family allows researchers greater freedom to move in the direction of understanding the strengths and coping strategies that the Black family has used to survive through successive cycles of formation and reformation, the family's role in preserving the Black heritage, and the way the supportive family network contributes to the growth and development of its members throughout the life cycle. At the applied level it is essential that social service agencies operating in the Black community reorganize their thinking about what constitutes a family in ways that will facilitate the delivery of a more comprehensive, well-coordinated package of services designed to strengthen the extended family and its support systems, rather than contributing to the breakup of the extended family by using a restrictive system of administrative rules based on the single-parent, subnuclear family.

Through discussion groups, workshops, and community forums, Black couples need to be provided with opportunities to look at the impact of cultural values on their relationship strategies, expectations, and goals, and to examine to what extent their values are congruent with the Afro-American ethos of genuineness, mutual aid, and interdependence. Finally, the nature of family life is changing in American society. With the advent of working mothers, rising divorce rates, and changing concepts of psychosexual roles, the family is moving outside the isolated nuclear framework for support systems and resource networks to assist with the concerns of living and child rearing. In developing alternative approaches to cope with the concerns of families in the contemporary era, a great deal can be learned from the cooperative and interdependent strategies that have been successful within the Black extended family.

REFERENCES

BALDWIN, JAMES. *The First Next Time.* New York: Dial Press, 1963.

BLASSINGAME, JOHN. *The Slave Community.* New York: Oxford University Press, 1972.

DUNBAR, PAUL LAURENCE. *The Complete Poems of Paul Laurence Dunbar.* New York: Dodd, Mead and Company, Inc., 1968.

ELKINS, STANLEY. *Slavery: A Problem in American Institutions and Intellectual Life.* Chicago: University of Chicago Press, 1968.

FRAZIER, E. FRANKLIN. *The Negro Family in the United States.* Chicago: University of Chicago Press, 1939.

FRANKLIN, ARETHA. *Aretha's Gold.* New York: Atlantic Records, 1969.

FREDRICKSON, GEORGE. "The Gutman Report," *The New York Review,* September 30, 1976, pp. 18–22, 27.

GUTMAN, HERBERT. *The Black Family in Slavery and Freedom, 1750–1925.* New York: Vintage Books, 1976.

KING, MARTIN LUTHER, JR. *Stride Toward Freedom.* New York: Harper & Row, 1958.

————. "I Have a Dream." Speech delivered at the March on Washington, August 28, 1963. In "We Shall Overcome," authorized recording produced by the Council for United Civil Rights Leadership.

LASCH, CHRISTOPHER. *The Culture of Narcissism.* New York: W. W. Norton, & Co., 1979.

LEVINE, LAWRENCE. *Black Culture and Black Consciousness.* New York: Oxford University Press, 1977.

McADOO, HARRIET, "Black Kinship," *Psychology Today,* May 1979, pp. 67–69, 79, 110.

MOYNIHAN, DANIEL PATRICK. *The Negro Family: The Case for National Action.* Washington, D.C.: U.S. Government Printing Office, 1965.

NOBLES, WADE. "Africanity: Its Role in Black Families," *The Black Scholar,* June 1974, pp. 10–17.

————. "Black People in White Insanity: An Issue for Community Mental Health," *Journal of Afro-American Issues,* 4, no. 1, (1976), 21–27.

————. "Toward an Empirical and Theoretical Framework for Defining Black Families," *Journal of Marriage and Family*, November 1978, pp. 679–688.

POWELL, ADAM CLAYTON, JR. *Marching Blacks*. New York: Dial Press, 1945

RAINWATER, LEE. *Behind Ghetto Walls: Black Family Life in a Federal Slum* Chicago: Aldine, 1970.

RAWLS, LOU. "Love is a Hurtin' Thing," from the album, *Lou Rawls Soulin'* (SM2566). Hollywood:

ROGERS, DOROTHY. *Adolescence: A Psychological Perspective*, 2nd Edition. Monterey, Calif.: Brooks/Cole, 1978.

SHANGE, NTOZAKE. *For Colored Girls Who Have Considered Suicide When the Rainbow is Enuf*. New York: Macmillan, 1977.

SHEEHY, GAIL. *Passages: Predictable Crisis of Adult Life*. New York Bantam, 1977.

SMITHERMAN, GENEVA. *Talkin and Testifyin: The Language of Black America*. Boston: Houghton Mifflin, 1977.

SOUTHERN, EILEEN. *The Music of Black Americans: A History*. New York: W. W. Norton and Co., 1971.

STACK, CAROL. *All Our Kin: Strategies for Survival in a Black Community*. New York: Harper & Row, 1974.

WALKER, MARGARET. *For My People*. New Haven: Yale University Press, 1942.

WALLACE, MICHELE. *Black Macho and the Myth of the Super Woman*. New York: Dial Press, 1979.

WEATHERS, DIANE. "A New Black Struggle," *Newsweek*, August 27, 1979, pp. 58–60.

CHAPTER FOUR

STAGES IN THE PSYCHOLOGICAL DEVELOPMENT OF BLACK YOUTH

INTRODUCTION

In the composite picture of Black children depicted in the writings of Ladner (1971), Coles (1972), White (1970), Herndon (1965), Joseph (1969), Brown (1966), and Gottlieb (1964), the youngsters are described as energetic, resourceful, innovative, clever, psychologically tough, self-confident, ambitious, and pensive. They are aware of the hardships and difficult realities that surround them, yet determined to create a brighter tomorrow by surging ahead with a sense of vitality to meet the challenges of life. Robert Coles captures the flavor of the emotional and psychological strengths of Black youth in his interviews with a young man who at nine years of age was one of only thirteen Blacks to integrate an all-white New Orleans elementary school in 1964 against substantial resistance. At the beginning of the experience he told Coles:

> I'm doing okay. Yes, I am. We stick together. So long as we can spot each other one or two times a day, we're all in good shape. But if I had to be the only one in school, with all the whites there—well, I'd still be willing to go. We've got to fight for our rights. I hope that when I'm a man I'm really a man. I hope I don't sit around waiting for some bossman to smile down on me and pat me on the head—or kick me in the pants. Some other kids, my own cousins—they're too good: They say white people don't mean us harm, and we should be nice to them, and they'll be nice to us. I laugh out loud when I hear them talking like that. They ask me why I go to the white school if I'm so against the white man, and I tell them that I want to learn all I can, and I want to

see what they're like, kids who will be wanting to boss us around in a few years when they're bigger. Then maybe I'll be wise enough about them to fool them; they've been tricking us ever since they brought us over here, and it's about time we learned to get even with them. My big brother says he wishes he had the chance; he wishes he could have gone to school with whites. If he'd gone, he thinks he'd be better off today. He'd be up to the whites. He'd know their number. I hope in a few years I won't be sitting around feeling regrets, like he does now. I hope I'll be in the ring, fighting it out with the Man. Our minister always says life is a boxing match, and he's right.

Six years later as a fifteen-year-old adolescent, he thought about the past and reflected on the future:

I have to stop and think every once in a while, and when I do I catch myself remembering the first few days—when I came to that school and suddenly found myself surrounded by white kids. I was scared I guess. I didn't feel scared then, but as I think back to those days, I was. The weather is changing you know; I realize that now. There's a different climate now between the races. The white people have to watch their step, just like we've always had to watch our step. It used to be the sun always shined on them and was raining on us. Now we've got some of the sun and they some rain. That's what I believe. So far as I'm concerned, I'm pretty hopeful. When I was a kid I used to fear growing up. I'd look at my big brother and my uncle, and I'd think of how my daddy died—in jail, because a white man hit him and then called the police and got them to arrest my daddy, and not the white man—and I'd get low, real low. I'd think to myself: There's no good life ahead for a colored boy like you.

But I'm not a colored boy. I'm a black man. Not all my people really grow up to be black men and black women. A lot of us are still colored; we're still niggers, or if we have a little money but no respect for ourselves, we're Negroes. To be black you have to feel you're going to get somewhere, and no one's going to stop you, no sir. A while back I used to have a dream, a nightmare, that there was a tornado coming up, like the kind that killed my granddaddy. I would be standing there, a little colored boy, I guess, and soon I'd be gone. I'd wake up thinking I was dead and gone, and expecting to see my granddaddy who is in his grave, near where the tornado killed him. I don't have the dream anymore. After studying in school and playing basketball and studying some more and working and trying to hold on to my girl—well, no wonder I fall into bed and the next thing I know it's morning, and I've never had a thing to dream about. If I did dream I think there'd be no tornadoes. Since I've gotten older I believe I've become more optimistic: I think I'll be able to do all right. I think the weather ahead will be pretty good. Actually, the weather has been getting better and better the last few years, and I guess I picked the right time to be born and to grow up.[1]

This composite picture reflecting the strengths of Black children is at variance with the retarded growth, negative self-image of Black children portrayed in the deficit-deficiency model. The purpose of this chapter is not to rehash the critique of the deficit-deficiency model but to trace the development of the strengths in Black children by looking at the socialization process from an Afro-American psychological perspective.

The Black child moves through the major stages of human growth and development within a sociocultural framework provided by the extended family. Since Black children are both human beings and American citizens, they share a common pattern of growth stages and developmental tasks with Euro-American children in the transition from early childhood to adulthood. There are, however, substantial differences between Black children and middle-class white children in terms of where the emphasis is placed in the periods of early childhood, middle childhood, preadolescence, early and middle adolescence, and young adulthood. During these critical developmental periods the focus for the Black child is successively on physical closeness, survival, mastery of the oral tradition, coming to grips with oppression, and resolving the inclusion–exclusion identity dilemma. In each critical developmental period the child is presented with a set of major psychosocial experiences requiring active mastery.

THE EARLY YEARS—
THE PRIMARY-CARE
AND MOTHERING PROCESS

The extended family makes available a number of adults, grandmothers, big mamas, and mother dears, plus older brothers and sisters who can assist the mother in the primary care of the infant, toddler, and preschool child. In a cultural framework that stresses

[1]Reprinted by permission of *Daedalus*, Journal of the American Academy of Arts and Sciences, Fall 1977, Boston, MA.

interdependence, emotional closeness, and physical touching, young children are likely to be given considerable affection, nurturance, and comforting physical contact (Kunkel and Kennaid, 1971). This prizing and caring from others generates a sense of confidence in the child that facilitates the unfolding of exploratory behaviors and curiosity drives. The child feels good about himself or herself, feels a basic trust in the early social milieu, and is willing to reach out through trial-and-error behavior to explore the world. The interactive effect between the natural epigenetic growth processes and the child's exploratory behavior produces an active mastery in the normal range of preschool developmental tasks. Black preschoolers learn how to walk, talk, go to the bathroom, dress themselves, and distinguish rudimentary cognitive concepts such as up–down, left–right, backward–forward, before–after, and basic counting without any apparent difficulty.

Supportive evidence for the assertion that Black preschool children are on schedule in sensory, motor, and cognitive development and in the development of self-esteem comes from the research of Bridgeman and Shipman (1975) and Mercer (1973, 1975). These researchers avoided the deficit-deprivation findings of earlier investigation by assessing the developmental mastery of children with multidimensional assessment techniques and with instruments that were relatively free of known cultural bias.

The active mastery of the primary developmental sensory, motor, and cognitive competencies during the first six years, reinforced by the approval of the extended family, strengthens the child's confidence and trust in self and others. The child's own sense of efficacy combined with love and support from the extended family becomes the basis for the development of a positive self-image. The self-images of Black children are not likely to be weighted down with the excessive feelings of guilt and shame. In a sociocultural framework where authenticity, openness to feelings, and spontaneity are encouraged, children are not taught to repress large parts of themselves as human beings in terms of a good me–bad me self concept. Although self-concept research on Black children has produced controversial findings, Taylor (1976), in reviewing the empirical research on self-concept and self-esteem in Black children, concluded that Black children have as much self-esteem as white children. He also noted that self-esteem in Black children is determined primarily by contacts within the Black family and community rather than by the negative imagery of Blackness in Euro-American culture. Taylor's findings are supported by the studies of Banks (1976), Kunkel and Kennaid (1971), and Bridgeman and Shipman (1975).

LEARNING SURVIVAL, RESPONSIBILITY, AND RESOURCEFULNESS

Children who grow up in the Black extended family are exposed to a cultural tradition where the emphasis is on survival through collective responsibility, resourcefulness, and resilience. In this network of interdependent human relationships, children learn by imitation, discovery, and direct teaching that they are expected to work cooperatively with others to make a contribution toward the survival and well-being of the group.

From the plantation to the contemporary urban community, successive generations of Black children have assisted their parents in caring for the sick, elderly, and shut-in and have assumed a major responsibility for taking care of younger brothers and sisters, preparing meals, doing housework, shopping for groceries, running errands, repairing broken appliances, and killing rats. The advent of working mothers in the Euro-American society has created concern about the so-called latch-key kids. These are white children who have the responsibility of looking out for themselves in the hours after school and when their parents either leave or arrive home from work. The term *latch key* comes from a custom in the past where children used to carry the key to the latch (lock) of the family residence on a string around their neck. Articles are appearing in periodicals and women's magazines about how to teach children to take care of theselves by dressing for school in presentable clothes, helping with the household chores, doing comparison shopping, cooking, and the like. There are minicourses designed to help these children learn "domestic survival" skills ("Survival Training," 1980).

The fact that Black children are past masters at this sort of survival learning went largely unnoticed. Little concern was expressed about the desirability of having children develop domestic survival skills until the situation began to have adverse effects on children of white, middle-class working mothers.

Black children have contributed economically to the family by working outside the home alongside parents, relatives, and other neighborhood adults in a variety of what sports commentator and former basketball star Bill Russell (1979) calls Negro jobs, such as cleaning office buildings, day work in white folks homes, picking cotton, delivering daily bets on numbers to local bankers, hauling coal, shining shoes, washing cars, and running errands for pimps, prostitutes, bookies, bootleggers, and other street hustlers. The children are well aware of how their efforts can contribute to improving the economic and psychological quality of life by relieving some of the stress on the adults, and responsible behavior is reinforced and rewarded.

Survival skills and adaptive behaviors are also learned by Black children in coping with the environment of the streets and with the army of social service authorities on children who monitor the Black community. Children have to cope with pressures from gangs, lunch-money shakedowns, and getting to and from school in deteriorating neighborhoods plagued by high incidences of homicides, assaults, armed robbery, alcoholism, and drug activities. They are confronted with major decisions about sex, drugs, theft, and physical combat much earlier than their white suburban counterparts. In *Man-Child in the Promised Land,* Claude Brown (1966) vividly describes what it was like as a Black youth to grow up in the streets of urban America. Not only must a child attempt to survive the streets, but they are constantly trying to evade child welfare workers, school authorities and attendance personnel, and juvenile police officers. While these officials might mean well, they have very little awareness of how the world appears to Black children.

In previous generations Black youth had to learn to work their way around adamant, southern racists represented by sheriffs, Klan members, white citizen council members, cotton field bosses, and plain ol' redneck crackers. They had to learn how to deal with these folks deceptively to get what they wanted without offending them. Coping with some of these southern white folks was literally a life-and-death issue. The young civil rights workers from the Student Nonviolent Coordinating Committee (SNICK) made up a medley of songs about not turning back in the face of beatings, jailings, and lynchings perpetrated by Southern white folks.

Children learn from first-hand experience that life is not always easy. They bear witness to their parents' confronting life situations that involve job layoffs, economic hardships, difficulties finding adequate housing, and sick loved ones—problems for which there are no simple, fairy-talelike solutions. They observe not only the specific strategies that adults use to cope with a host of difficult situations, but more important, the general demeanor of vitality, resilience, and resourcefulness Black folks express as they keep on keepin' on in the face of the ups and downs of life. They learn the difference between being disappointed and being destroyed. Internalizing this generalized attitude of resilience fortifies the child against feelings of despair, apathy, and vulnerability.

The resourcefulness and problem-solving skills that the children are learning shows up in the inventiveness and creativity of their play activities. From the Mississippi Delta to the streets of Watts, poor Black children fashion toys and sports equipment out of cast-off furniture, junk, old tires, and fruit cartons. Ghetto children are constantly inventing new games emphasizing group participation and adding parts to existing games. The survival training the youngster receives inside and outside the family circle stimulates the development of thought processes associated with problem-solving skills. The children are learning the conceptual processes involved in decision-making strategies: how to size up a situation, figure out the alternatives, anticipate the consequences, and plan ahead to avoid disastrous results. Black children who have developed these decision-making, coping, and problem-solving abilities have amassed a rich pool of learning skills with respect to how to break things down, organize their thoughts, and take care of business by carrying out an appropriate course of action. Somehow, educators are unable to tap these skills as a foundation for building academic competencies.

MASTERY OF LANGUAGE
AND THE ORAL TRADITION

Mastering the intricacies and nuances of Black language and the oral tradition represents a way for the preadolescent and early adolescent youth to increase their awareness of the Black heritage, improve their interpersonal skills, enhance their effectiveness in dealing with group dynamics, and sharpen their conceptual skills. By tuning in to the oral information banks in the Black community, teenagers can find out what went on in the past, what's going on now, and what is likely to go on in the future. Information about social events, jobs, what's happening, who to trust, hip parties, together teachers, educational opportunities, and rumbles, in keeping with the oral tradition, is carried across the social networks in the Black community on the grapevine.

The spoken word is an influential force within the Black community. Social interaction is conducted through an elaborate system of sociolinguistic codes and categories. To increase their range of participation in social interaction and interpersonal relationships, youngsters must learn how and when to signify, play the dozens, sweet talk, cap, bad mouth, testify, rhapsodize, and woof. Running it down and talking that talk in a language system that requires an active call–response interaction between speaker and listener demands a certain kind of social perceptiveness, mental alertness,and linguistic inventiveness. In order to be in time with the tempo, pace, and flow of what's going down verbally, the youngster has to understand the subtle meaning of figures of speech, catch phrases, and opening statements while interchanging roles as speaker and listener. In a fast-moving dialogue the youngster's meanings have to be deciphered quickly and instant decisions have to be made about when to fire on somebody, when to keep cool, and when to cosign. When one youngster says to another, "I saw Jo the other night," it is implicitly understood by the group that this is an invitation to play the dozens. What the term "Jo" refers to is the recipient's mother: "Jo-who?" "Jo mama." If the recipient answers by saying "What goes around, comes around," this is understood as meaning, "Be sure you know what you're gettin' ready to get into, 'cause I'm gettin' ready to drop a whole lot about what your mama's been doin' on you that you sho' 'nough don't want to hear." A "bad rap"[2] will get you over in the Black community, especially when it comes to adolescents initiating contact with members of the opposite sex.

While taking part in these verbal interchanges, Black youngsters become adept at using analogies, metaphors, double entendres, and Black figures of speech to express complex relationships between objects, events, concepts, and ideas (Holt, 1975). These linguistic manipulations build up the child's capacity for abstract thinking and logical reasoning. Embedded within the language system of the Black community is an auditory–oral learning style based on participatory interaction. In the call–response dialogue young people learn how to understand ideas, recognize conceptual relationships, and gain information about what's happening in the world around them by listening to the message from the speaker, decoding it, and verbally responding to what is interpreted as the essence of the message. The reply from the listener triggers a subsequent feedback response from the original speaker to indicate whether or not the listener understood the initial message.

DISCOVERING AND COPING WITH OPPRESSION

Long before the child can verbalize, he or she is aware of the fact that something is fundamentally wrong in the American society, that some pervasive, catastrophic, oppressive force is preventing Black folks from achieving their goals and participating in the range of opportunities that America provides for its citizens (Baldwin, 1963). The complete impact of this awareness does not come all at once but falls into place gradually during middle childhood, preadolescence, and early adolescence. As the child looks into the mirror image of society reflected in TV, movies, newspapers, and stories about the heroes of American history, he or she sees white folks projected with imagery of power, courage, competence, beauty, and goodness. Listening to parents and other adults within the extended family

[2]An effective, colorful, dynamic speaker—one who uses such speech.

networks, he or she hears about how white folks have control over jobs, the prices of food, rent, and wages, the length of jail sentences. He or she hears how white folks have provided one after another stumbling block to make life difficult for Black folks. The child may hear tales of earlier times down South when white folks blatantly denied the civil rights of Black folks by lynch mobs, states rights, and Jim Crow laws operating within a separate but never equal social system. Black children and youth cannot avoid the unmistakable conclusion that white folks have a freer access to high-paying jobs and positions of influence and a reasonable opportunity to utilize whatever marketable skills they develop.

The conclusion that racism is pervasive in the American society has a profound and lasting influence on the Black young people. They may express their disappointment with anger, fear, resentment, or bitterness. It cannot help but generate a period of confusion in Black youth, because it forces them to deal with contradictions that have been inherent in American society for over 350 years. On the one hand, the child has heard that this is the land of equal opportunity, liberty, and justice for all, and that all humans are created equal and endowed by their creator with certain inalienable rights. Yet, the reality of experience has made the child aware of the fact that this is definitely not the case.

There are no easy answers to this quandary. Black youth want the opportunities whites have in terms of power, influence, freedom to grow and develop, adequate health care, decent housing, and no police harassment. This does not, however, mean that Black young people want to be white. In fact, they may hold a very low opinion of whites as human beings. Just as the youth has heard about white power and dominance, he or she has also heard white folks described in derisive terms as honkies, redneck crackers, paddies, peckerwoods, fay boys, white boys, and Charlies, with the bottom line from the Black culture being that they can't be trusted. Furthermore, the adolescent may feel, based on personal contacts with white folks, that they are dull, boring, and talk differently. There is a difference between wanting the choices the oppressors have and identifying with the oppressors in terms of being dependent on their approval in defining one's personal worth. Rather, for affirmation of their personal worth and help in sorting out contradictory impressions of social reality, Black youth are likely to turn to the Black folks who have nurtured and supported them from their early years. Through this network of family and peers in the immediate psychosocial milieu of the Black community, young people establish a frame of reference to filter conflicting impressions from the white world (Taylor, 1976). The premise that Black youth filter their impressions of the white world and establish their sense of worth through a Black frame of reference was not sufficiently considered by the deficit-deficiency writers in their assumption that Blacks had internalized an image of self-hatred.

Black youth attempt to combat the economic, psychological, and social effects of oppression by using a variety of strategies. Adolescents may go through periods of denial, periods where they feel the effects of racism won't touch them and that they will get away clean if they follow the Euro-American values of hard work and future orientation. Some youth become involved with gang activities, fighting, bubble-gum pimping, nickel-and-dime hustling, theft, drugs, sporadic school attendance, and streetcorner crime that brings them to the attention of juvenile authorities. These so-called experts cannot seem to understand that the seemingly illegal and sometimes violent behavior of Black youth may be a form of social protest against the forces that have created deteriorating inner city neighborhoods.

Many youth try to concentrate on developing a gimmick or a "stick," some area of super mastery they hope to use to increase their range of mainstream options (Baldwin, 1963; Malcolm X, 1965). Sports, the performing arts, oratorical skills, cooking, mechanical skills, and even academic achievement represent major areas of excellence that Black youth feel will provide them with the opportunity to increase their range of options. The Black community is alive with youngsters trying to get their act together, do their thing, and perfect the moves of their particular game with glamour, grace, and style. While only a few reach the top as professional athletes, singers, movies actors, jet pilots, preachers, teachers, doctors, and engineers, the mastery experiences that these young people develop in pursuing these "sticks" build confidence in their ability to learn by providing them with concrete evidence of their talents. If Black youth are going to have an equivalent range of choices during their lifetimes it will in large measure depend on their ability to create new pathways around existing socioeconomic problems. This being the case, it is essential that Black youth develop the capacity to be resourceful, imaginative, and innovative.

The survival orientation, responsibility-taking behaviors, problem-solving skills, self-confidence, and resilient attitutde that the Black adolescent has already started to incorporate during the preadolescent years will help in the effort to put together a stick to combat the limited range of options, protect him or her from a sense of despair during the inevitable setbacks, and enable him or her to keep on keepin' on until a workable range of options emerges. Black adolescents who have not sufficiently internalized the protective and energizing features of the Afro-American ethos will be vulnerable to feelings of futility, despair, and doubt about their own worth as human beings, feelings that can prevent the healthy resolution of issues associated with establishing a solid identity.

IDENTITY CONFLICTS

During late adolescence and early adulthood Black youth, like other American youth, struggle with major decisions about what to do with their lives, where they are going, how they are going to get there, how to get a piece of the economic action and political power, and what is important to them in the way of values, standards, and ideals. In seeking to come to grips with these identity-related issues, Black youth cannot completely avoid the reality of the social contradictions inherent in American life. Those who have been protected from the reality of social contradictions are going to come into contact with other Blacks at this stage; they cannot be permanently sealed off from the fact of oppression in American life.

One of the major decisions confronting Black youth involves preparation for the world of work. While high school counselors, social workers, college recruiters, and representatives of skilled trades paint an optimal picture of a future supported by affirmative action opportunities, the Black adolescent, considering America's past performance, has no reasonable guarantee that these programs will last. Equal access to quality employment has never been a reality in Black America. The number of unemployed and underemployed people Black youth see everyday in Black neighborhoods bears witness to the fact that hard work has not made the American dream come to pass to Black folks. Black people have worked from sun-up to sun-down picking cotton, sharecropping, cleaning white folk's houses, washing their clothing, laying rails, and working on chain gangs. They have no trouble at all believing Stokely Carmichael (1971) when he used to say that if hard work paid off, Black people would be the richest people in America, they would own this country "lock-stock-and-barrel, from top to bottom, left to right."

Black youth have to decide whether or not they will invest their time and energies developing competencies and skills that the society may not allow them to utilize fully. It is important for people who work with Black youth to understand that the youth see beyond tokenism, entry-level jobs, make-work jobs, and the like. They want a shot at the whole range of opportunities that exist within American society, and without the visibility of concrete Black role models in every decision-making arena of the economic, political and governmental spectrum, no amount of telling them about hard work, sacrifice, patience, and things getting better will convince them that equal opportunity in America is really a solid thing. The decision to pursue a medium to long-range course of action designed to develop marketable mainstream skills comes down to whether or not the youngster is willing to take a risk. The risk is more than economic; it also involves the youngster's emotional well-being. If youngsters invest this time and effort and it doesn't pay off, they will face a profound setback. The Black community is filled with society's economic rejects from previous generations, super-talented brothers and sisters, now junkies, addicts, ex-offenders, and low-echelon government workers whose ambitions were destroyed by the structural racism built into the system. The alternative to taking this high-stakes risk is to say "the hell with it" and not to waste time and energies pursuing an improbable dream.

Young adults are confronted with a set of dualities defined by being part of, yet apart from, American society, in it but not of it, included at some levels and excluded at others. This duality is at the heart of the identity struggle and generates powerful feelings of rage and indignation. The inclusion–exclusion dilemma is further complicated by their exposure to two different value systems, world views, and historical legacies. In the *Souls of Black Folks,* DuBois (1903) spoke of this cultural and historical duality as a kind of two-ness, a double consciousness created by a confluence of Afro-American and Euro-American, Black and white realities going on inside of him at the same time. Others have used terms such as double vision (Wright, 1953), bicultural (Valentine, 1968), diunital (Dixon and Foster, 1971), and multidimensional (Cross, 1980) to describe the double consciousness experience.

Each Black adolescent must attempt to set up some workable balance between Afro-American and Euro-American values within his or her own life space. Complete denial of either frame of reference will restrict choices in personal growth, interpersonal relationships, and economic opportunities. If the individual concentrates solely on a life style that emphasizes individualism, competition, emotional insulation, power, dominance, and control, he or she may achieve success at the cost of being alienated from Black peers and elders who value genuineness, mutual aid, and emotional closeness. On the other hand, if the young adult completely ignores those values that will allow progress in the occupational mainstream, he or she will have dramatically reduced the available range of options, and the material quality of life associated with these options. These difficult decisions about value orientations occur at a time when young adults are consolidating their sexual identity and trying to establish guidelines and expectations for intimate relationships.

The search for a viable combination of values that will result in a productive and emotionally satisfying life style can prove to be elusive. Like the protagonist without a name in Ralph Ellison's *Invisible Man* (1952), the Black young adult may go through a series of major role changes accompanied by defeat, disillusionment, and disappointment before understanding that the only solid answers come through direct experience. Young adults may go through changes where they think they are much smarter than their low-middle-income Black parents, where they believe that Black folks don't have much to offer, where they are convinced that they can escape oppression by hard work, courage, and a commitment to excellence. The periods where they feel that they are going to get away clean can be followed by periods of disillusionment, which are reflected in superblackness, supermilitancy, and blanket rejection of honkies. The resolution of the identity conflict begins when the young adult finally understands, regardless of whatever combination of Euro-American and Afro-American values is chosen or whatever life style is selected, that the proverbial wisdom contained in the Black folk culture can contribute meaning, beauty, and enrichment to life. If the person lives long enough, they will come to realize that "you cannot make it in this world alone," that "you better be yourself or you gonna be by yourself," that "love is a hurtin' thing," that compassion is more productive than guilt and shame, that feeling good, getting happy, and getting down are an essential part of the revitalization process necessary to overcome defeat, that "you can't lie to life," that "what's goes around comes around," and that in the end "the man will reap what he has sown."

As young adults continue their journey through the contingencies of the adult life cycle, they will, like James Baldwin (1955), discover and rediscover the value of the Afro-American ethos as a potential source of strength and guidance. Internalization of the substance of the Afro-American world view, transmitted by the tribal elders through the oral tradition, will enable them to keep the faith and keep on climbin'. This does not happen all at once but comes together gradually as children progress sequentially from the early nurturant years in the extended family through survival learning, mastery of the oral tradition, discovering and coping with oppression, and the resolution of identity conflicts.

REFERENCES

BALDWIN, JAMES. *Notes of a Native Son*. New York: Bantam Books, 1955.
————. *The Fire Next Time*. New York: Dell Publishing Co., 1963.
BANKS, W. C. "White Preference in Blacks: A Paradigm in Search of a Phenomenon," *Psychological Bulletin*, 83 (1976), 1179–1186.
BRIDGEMAN, B., and SHIPMAN, V. C. *Disadvantaged Children and Their First School Experience*. Report Prepared For Project Head Start. Washington, D.C.: Office of Child Development, 1975.

BROWN, CLAUDE. *Man-Child in the Promised Land.* New York: Signet Books, 1966.

CARMICHAEL, STOKELY. *Stokely Speaks, Black Power Back to Pan-Africanism.* New York: Vintage Books, 1971.

COLES, ROBERT. *Farewell to the South.* Boston: Little, Brown, 1972.

CROSS, WILLIAM. "Models of Psychological Nigrescence: A Literature Review," in R. L. Jones ed., *Black Psychology* 2nd ed. New York: Harper & Row, 1980.

DIXON, V., and FOSTER, B. *Beyond Black or White.* Boston: Little, Brown, 1971.

DuBois, W. E. B. *The Souls of Black Folk.* Chicago: McClurg, 1903.

ELLISON, RALPH. *Invisible Man.* New York: Random House, 1952.

FREEDOM SINGERS. *The Freedom Singers Sing of Freedom Now* (#60924/MG20924). New York: Mercury Record Corp., 1964.

GOTTLIEB, DAVID. "Teaching and Students: The Views of Negro and White Teachers," *Sociology of Education,* 37 (Summer 1964) 345–353.

HERNDON, JAMES. *The Way It Spozed To Be.* New York: Bantam Books, 1965.

HOLT, GRACE. "Metaphor, Black Discourse Style, and Cultural Reality," in Robert L. Williams, ed., *Ebonics: The True Language of Black Folks.* St. Louis: Institute of Black Studies, 1975.

JOSEPH, STEPHEN M. *The Me Nobody Knows: Children's Voices from the Ghetto.* New York: Avon Books, 1969.

KUNKEL, P., and KENNAID, A. *Sprout Spring, A Black Community.* New York: Holt, Rinehart & Winston, 1971.

LADNER, JOYCE A. *Tomorrow's Tomorrow: The Black Woman.* New York: Doubleday, 1971.

MALCOLM X. *The Autobiography of Malcolm X.* New York: Grove Press, 1965.

MERCER, JANE R. *Labeling the Mentally Retarded.* Berkeley University of California Press, 1973.

———. "Sociocultural Factors in Educational Labeling," pp. 141–157 in M. J. Begab and S. A. Richardson, eds., *The Mentally Retarded and Society: A Social Science Perspective.* Baltimore: University Park Press, 1975.

RUSSELL, BILL, and BRANCH, TAYLOR. *Second Wind: The Memoirs of an Opinionated Man.* New York: Random House, 1979.

"Survival Training for Latchkey Kids," *Newsweek,* October 6, 1980, p. 100.

TAYLOR, R. L. "Psychosocial Development Among Black Children and Youth: A Re-examination," *American Journal of Orthopsychiatry,* 46 (January 1976), 4–19.

VALENTINE, CHARLES A. *Culture and Poverty.* Chicago: University of Chicago Press, 1968.

WHITE, JOSEPH. "Toward a Black Psychology," *Ebony,* September 1970, pp. 44–45, 48–50, 52.

WRIGHT, RICHARD. *The Outsider,* New York: Harper & Row, 1953.

CHAPTER FIVE

TEACHING BLACK YOUTH: AN EDUCATIONAL PSYCHOLOGY

STATEMENT OF THE PROBLEM

The situation confronting Black children in the American educational scene is a dismal picture of failure. Repeated observations of Black children have shown that once they enter school they fall quickly behind their white counterparts on measurements of intelligence, achievement, and scholastic attainment (Clark, 1965; Coleman, 1966; Fogelson, 1969; Denton, 1981). This academic lag occurs despite the fact that when Black children enter school they know how to walk, talk, and appear to have mastered the preschool sensory, motor, and cognitive skills (Bridgeman and Shipman, 1975). The longer Black children remain on the educational conveyor belt, the further they fall behind. Their measured IQ and achievement levels decrease with the length of time they stay in school; interpreted literally this would mean that the longer they stay in school, the less intellectually able they become.

Citing statistics compiled from the U.S. Census Bureau data submitted in a report by the Children's Defense Fund, a Washington-based lobby and advocacy group for children, Denton (1981) states that compared to white children, Black children are three times as likely to be labeled as mentally retarded, are twice as likely to be suspended for discipline and attendance problems, and are twice as likely to drop out of high school before the twelfth grade. Those who remain in school are anywhere from two to three years below grade level in reading, math, and elementary science. Dropouts and those who graduate from high school without any appreciable mastery of basic educational competencies rapidly become incorporated in the unemployment, welfare, and law enforcement statistics that plague Black urban communities. Despite the remedial education programs and social reform movements of the 1960s and 1970s, Black children have only half as much of a chance as a white child of finishing college and becoming a professional person, and twice as much chance of being unemployed in adulthood. They have a one-in-ten chance of getting into trouble with the law and a five-year shorter life expectancy than a white.

Two complementary deficit-deficiency hypotheses, genetic inferiority and cultural deprivation, have been advanced by American laypersons, psychologists, and educators to account for the plight of Black children in the nation's school systems.

The genetic inferiority hypothesis, supported by traditional American folklore of Anglo superiority, has been championed in each decade of the twentieth century by a well-known Euro-American psychologist: G. Stanley Hall and Henry Goddard in the period between the turn of the century and World War I; Robert Yerkes in the 1920s; Louis Terman in the 1930s; Henry Garrett in the 1940s; Carl Brigham in the 1950s; and Arthur Jensen in the 1960s and 1970s (Franklin, 1980; Block and Dworkin, 1976). The popular belief in Black inferiority was backed up by the weight and legitimacy of science.

In the liberal tradition of the New Frontier and Great Society of the 1960s, America's educational reformers, at least in public, broke away from the genetic inferiority position. Cultural deprivation replaced hereditary deficit as an explanation for the failure cycle of Black children in the country's educational enterprise. According to the point of view espoused in the theory of the culturally deprived child (Deutsch, 1967; Riessman, 1962), the Black child's family and community are unable to provide the proper background experiences and mental stimulation necessary for proper growth of the cognitive and perceptual skills associated with classroom learning.

The antidote for cultural deprivation was compensatory education (Hellmuth, 1970). The federal government sponsored a massive remediation program, costing the taxpayers millions of dollars, to enrich the backgrounds of culturally impoverished children. From pre-school to college, Black children were headstarted, upward-bounded, remediated, and specially admitted into higher educational horizons. The results of compensatory education's remedial-enrichment approach were by and large unsuccessful. After a decade of educational experimentation that began in the 1960s, the prognosis for Black youth remained questionable. In his article, "End of the Impossible Dream," written in the early 1970s, Peter Schrag (1970) attributes the failure of compensatory education to the lack of any substantive changes in educational philosophy, content, and instructional styles. There was no departure from the concern with orderliness, obedience, punctuality, drill, rote memory, and technical mastery of the three R's. No substantive changes occurred to make education more interesting and exciting by bringing into the classroom the learning styles, language, survival skills, expectations, and suspicions about the future the child brings to school from the Afro-American experience base.

The failure of compensatory education paved the way for the reappearance of genetic inferiority theories toward the end of the 1960s. After millions of dollars had been spent with no appreciable results, Euro-Americans were more willing to listen to the genetic inferiority theories proposed by Jensen (1969) and Shockley (1971).

The genetic inferiority and cultural deprivation hypothesis have in common the assignment of the blame for school failures to the child and the child's family, the former through inheritance of raggedy IQ genes and the latter through deficient environments. By assigning the blame to the children and their families, educators can avoid coming to grips with the problems of reconstructing the learning process in a way that draws out the strengths in the Black child's psychosocial background and cultural heritage.

An attempt will be made in this chapter to reconstruct the learning process as it relates to Black children by examining the four variables commonly associated with classroom learning: intelligence, achievement motivation, language, and the additive effect. Each of these four interrelated variables will be redefined from a learning perspective that capitalizes on the psychological and cultural strengths of the Black child.

INTELLIGENCE AND LEARNING: HISTORY AND CULTURAL BIAS

It is a commonly accepted principle in education that children with greater intelligence can be expected to learn more rapidly and achieve a higher level of academic mastery than children who are less intellectually endowed. The relationship between learning and intelligence is normally demonstrated by means of a positive statistical correlation in the neighborhood of 0.50 between scores on standardized intelligence tests and learning outcomes as measured by grades, achievement tests, and teacher ratings of the student's level of proficiency (Harlow, et al. 1971). The positive statistical relationship between scores on intelligence tests and academic performance should come as no surprise. Alfred Binet, whose pioneer work on intellectual assessment laid the foundation for the twentieth-century intelligence test and its derivatives in the form of scholastic aptitude and achievement tests, initially set out to build an assessment tool that would be useful in predicting school success.

To briefly review the historical events surrounding the development of the first Binet-Simon mental assessment scales published in 1905, Binet, the director of the Sorbonne Psychology Laboratory in Paris, and his associate Dr. Theodore Simon were hired by the French government in 1904 as consultants to assist with the problems of pupil placement in the public schools.[1] In 1904, fifteen years after compulsory education was introduced, the Paris schools were overcrowded. Slow students were holding up the progress of better ones. One solution was to identify those students who lacked either the mental capacity or scholastic readiness required by the standard curriculum and place them in special classes. Binet's assignment was to develop an assessment tool to identify those pupils whose academic aptitude or readiness was so slow as to require their placement in special classes. Binet and Simon had been working on the problems associated with intellectual assessment for over ten years when they were hired by the schools, and they had developed an exploratory battery of mental tests for children ages

---

[1]The History of Binet's Research presented herein was compiled from the following sources: Binet and Simon (1916); Stoddard (1943); Cronbach (1949).

three to eleven. In selecting test items for their work with the schools, they concentrated on those items from the exploratory battery that appeared to correspond to the activities required of students in the classroom. Binet and Simon reasoned that an item or task would be useful in predicting school success if it distinguished (discriminated) between bright and dull students. The students were classified into groups of bright and dull on the basis of teacher's judgments. For an item to be considered significant in terms of discriminating between bright and dull students, a larger percentage of the bright students at each age level had to be able to answer the item correctly. Test scores were expressed in terms of the relationship of mental age to chronological age. Children were considered above average if their mental age was higher than their chronological age and, conversely, below average if their mental age, was less than their chronological age.

The original 1905 Binet-Simon Intelligence Scale, revised in 1908, is saturated with items measuring such classroom-related activities as verbal reasoning, arithmetic, social comprehension, and general information. The explanation for the low positive correlation between school grades and IQ scores is straightforward; they are both measuring a common, school-related mastery factor. The structure of the IQ test, with its strong verbal-mathematical factor, has not changed since Binet. The original contents underwent many revisions in form but not in substance.

Binet cautioned against thinking of these mental age scores as representing any fixed, gene-carried, absolute measure of intelligence. He was against the idea of a fixed, innate intelligence and was not interested in making a distinction between acquired and congenital mental deficits. He thought of his test as a diagnostic instrument that could be used in school settings to identify children who needed special tutoring assistance in the form of what he referred to as mental orthopedics.

American psychologists rapidly incorporated the intelligence quotient as a primary measurement tool. Under the leadership of Stanford psychology professor Louis Terman, Binet's original test, after being translated from French to English in 1908 by Henry Goddard, a psychologist at New Jersey's Vineland Training School for the Feeble Minded, was restandardized using a normative sample of native-born American white children in 1916 and again in 1937 (Terman, 1916; Terman and Merrill, 1937). The American version of Binet's test, the Stanford-Binet, while retaining the concept of the mental age, allowed for a conversion of mental age scores into numbers, like points along a scale, that could be easily understood by professional educators and laymen alike. The average for all ages was designated by a convenient score of 100; scores above 115 were considered above average or bright normal, and scores under 85 were considered low average to borderline retarded (Cronbach, 1949).

The idea that mental ability could be measured by a standardized intelligence test and reported by a convenient numerical scoring system appealed to the objective, scientific orientation that was developing within American psychology. Terman (1916, 1923) and his colleagues championed the use of the IQ test as a scientifically valid method of classifying children in an educational system based on the principle of meritocracy. The most able American school children could be identified early and given the kind of education necessary to develop their superior talents. Intellectually talented children identified by the IQ test would be groomed as future leaders of America—a sort of power elite built on mental giftedness, reminiscent of Plato's philosopher-kings. Less talented children would be conditioned by teaching methods focusing on drill, rote memory, order, punctuality, and obedience to prepare them to fit easily into the lock-step routine of America's factories where they would work as adults (Karier, 1976). In Terman's philosophy those with IQs of 140 and above were not only thought to have superior intellectual endowment but were also considered to be of superior moral character. To put it bluntly, they were just better human beings than those with average and below average IQs.

As the mental abilities testing movement gained power and prominence in the first half of the twentieth century under the combined sponsorship of America's prestigious universities, philanthropic foundations, and government agencies, its leaders, apparently forgetting Binet's early warnings, seemed convinced that these IQ tests, originally validated on the basis of teacher judgment of brightness and dumbness, represented the child's permanent, inherited, gene-carried, intellectual endowment (Block and Dworkin, 1976). Except for minor errors of measurement, the IQ rating, once established, was not expected to change during the course of a lifetime. It was as if the IQ test came from the hand of Almighty God (Voyat, 1969).

From the beginning of the intelligence testing movement in America, studies indicated that Black children as a group tended to score ten to fifteen points lower than white children (Guthrie, 1976; Fincher, 1976). According to the classification system used by the intelligence testers, this would place Black children in the low normal to mildly retarded range. How to interpret this ten to fifteen-point difference, exactly what it means, and what causes it is part of a heated controversy that has been going on in psychology for the past seventy years. Several prominent Euro-American psychologists, as noted earlier, have accepted the Black-white difference in intelligence test scores as scientific evidence supporting the popular Anglo view that white folks, especially the descendants of Western–Nordic Europeans, are genetically superior in intelligence. Others argued against this conclusion of white superiority–Black inferiority; they pointed out that the intelligence test tended to favor a background of experiences more common to middle-class white children; therefore, middle-class white children should be expected to score higher (Franklin, 1980).

In reviewing the evidence on Black-white differences in IQ, Jensen (1969, 1980) and Herrnstein (1971, 1973) noted that for certain groups of Blacks, IQ scores had increased but were still not identical with those of whites. Among the groups that showed an increase were middle- and upper-middle-class Blacks, northern urban as compared to rural southern Blacks, and low-income Black children who were given special preschool experiences in programs such as Head Start. This was taken to mean that intelligence test scores could be improved with experience, but there still remained differences in favor of whites, which according to Jensen could only be accounted for by genetic differences between the races. Jensen, however, did not sufficiently address the question of how Black-white cultural differences in expressive patterns, language usage, conceptual styles, and problem-solving approaches could generate legitimate, equivalent alternative answers to the items on intelligence tests. While the controversy surrounding Black-white differences in IQ scores continued unabated, thousands of Black school children were being classified as mentally defective due to their low scores and placed in special classes for retarded youth.

Black educators, social scientists, and psychologists refused to accept these low IQ scores as a valid measure of the Black child's fixed, gene-carried intellectual ability. They expressed outrage at the irreparable harm being done to Black children by the practice of declaring them intellectually deficient on the basis of culturally biased assessment tools and placing them in classes for the educationally retarded. The history of the debate against the IQ tests by Black educators and psychologists is reviewed in Guthrie (1976) and Franklin (1980). The theoretical issues involved in their criticism are summarized in the two-sided "cultural mismatch" hypothesis presented by Williams (1974, 1975a). First, IQ tests were saturated with questions like, "What is a shilling?" which presume some familiarity with Anglo culture. Second, the Afro-American experiential and cultural perspective was not adequately represented in the test. The absence of an Afro-American cultural perspective caused answers that were correct from the Black child's frame of reference to be scored incorrect according to the norms of the test author. This type of cultural mismatch error can be illustrated by a hypothetical question asking the Black child to define the word "dust." Webster's Dictionary defines it as "fine, powdery particles of the earth." In the lexicon of the Black community "dust" means money (derived from gold dust), thus to the Black child, "The dude had big dust," means the person had a lot of money.

After many years of heated debate in the literature, at professional conferences, and in the media, Black psychologists, led by the Bay Area Association of Black Psychologists, selected the courts as a primary arena to present their case against cultural bias in the traditional IQ test. In the now-famous Larry P. case, the San Francisco Bay Area Black Psychology Association challenged the practice of using intelligence test scores as a valid method for placing Black children in classes for the mentally retarded. Larry P. (1972, 1979) was a class action suit filed on behalf of the plaintiff, Larry P., and five other Black students from the San Francisco Unified School District.

The Bay Area Association began their arguments with the

documented fact that Black children were disproportionately represented in the classes for mentally retarded youngsters and nearly absent in classes for the gifted (Aubrey, 1975). In 1971 Black students constituted 28.5 percent of the San Francisco school district's population, yet 60 percent of the pupils in the educable mentally retarded (EMR) classes were Black. Statewide in California there was even a larger discrepancy. Black students were 9.1 percent of the total school population and 27.5 percent of the population of EMR programs, nearly three times their numbers in the regular school population. The legal basis of the Black psychologist's challenge was the equal protection clause of the Fourteenth Amendment. Proceeding from the basic premise that intellectual talent was equally distributed across the races at birth, the psychologists and their attorneys argued that the San Francisco school district, by using culturally biased IQ tests to place disproportionate numbers of Black youngsters in classes for the mentally retarded, was interfering with the rights of these youngsters to pursue equal access to the quality of education offered by the mainstream classroom. They also stated that when children are unfairly labeled as mentally deficient by a public educational institution, a negative cycle of expectations is set into motion, a self-fulfilling prophesy that eventually destroys the confidence of children in their ability to learn. To support the charge of cultural bias, Black psychologists retested the six plaintiffs who had been labeled as retarded on the basis of IQ tests administered by the school district. The retesting was done by a Black examiner, and modifications were made in the scoring system to take into consideration cultural differences in the Black child's responses. Using the modified scoring criteria, answers that normally would have been scored wrong were scored correct if they made sense from the child's perspective and, as such, represented an effective solution to the problem as presented.

Presented below are two examples from this writer's experience in testing Black children that do not meet the test author's criteria for a correct response, yet make a great deal of sense from the perspective of the inner-city Black child. In response to the question, "What should you do if a child much smaller than you tries to start a fight with you?" a nine-year-old Black male gave the following answer: "I would hit him back, I don't be buyin' no woof (wolf) tickets and I don't be sellin' no woof tickets, buyin' woof tickets ain't nothin' but trouble." A fourteen-year-old Black youth when asked, "What should you do if you see a train approaching a broken track?" responded by saying, "I ain't gonna try to play no hero and hold up no red flag. If something goes wrong and I'm there, my probation officer will violate me and send me back to juvie, I'm gonna split as fast as I can." In each of these examples the youngster demonstrates a capacity for logical, sequential thinking by identifying the important elements in the situation, putting these elements together in a rational perspective, and choosing a solution that is consistent with his analysis of the problem. Anybody who has gone to an inner-city school knows that "if you be buyin' woof tickets it will get around the grapevine that you can be jacked up and little brothers and sisters will be steady kicking your ass."

When the plaintiffs were retested with this modified scoring system developed by Black psychologists, their IQ scores showed an increase of 17 to 38 points. All of the plaintiffs tested above 75, the cutoff scores by the San Francisco school district for placement in classes for the mentally retarded.

The rationale for the modified scoring system used in the Larry P. case was to reduce the white middle-class bias by incorporating the Afro-American experience base as a legitimate aspect of the IQ test. This rationale is based on the supposition that there is a range of intellectual skills, conceptual processes, language and expressive patterns, problem-solving approaches, and survival patterns characteristic of Afro-American life styles that are not assessed by the traditional IQ test or, for that matter, in school grades and other indices of academic achievement. Other promising alternatives for incorporating the Black experience base as a way of minimizing cultural bias include Blackanizing existing IQ tests and the Black Culture Specific test. In Blackanizing the existing IQ tests, a method proposed by Dr. Charles Thomas (1979), items are included that are specifically designed to require familiarity with the nuances of Afro-American culture: items such as, "What is the difference between *signifying* and *playing the dozens*?" or "What does this saying mean?" "What goes around comes around." The Black Culture Specific tests consists of an entire pool of items drawn from the Black experience base. The most widely known Black Cultural Specific test is the BITCH test, Black Intelligence Test of Cultural Homogeneity, devised by Robert Williams (1972a, 1972b) a nationally known expert on the use of intelligence tests with Blacks. The items on the BITCH test require the respondent to have some familiarity with terms such as *conk, jack-leg preacher, H.N.I.C. CPT, main squeeze,* and *boggie jugie.* Needless to say, many whites would score ten to fifteen points below Blacks on the BITCH test.

In a series of landmark decisions in the Larry P. case from 1972 to 1979, Chief U.S. District Court Judge Robert F. Peckham ruled that educational officials had violated the equal protection rights of the plaintiffs by using IQ tests to place an inordinate number of Black students in classes for the mentally retarded. In 1972 Judge Peckham issued an injunction ordering that no Black pupils in the San Francisco School District could be placed in classes for the mentally retarded on the basis of IQ test scores. This injunction was expanded in 1974 to cover the entire state of California, pending a final disposition in the San Francisco case. Finally, on October 16, 1979, Judge Peckham made permanent the ban he had issued in 1974 covering the entire state (Larry P., 1979; Hager, 1979). In a massive 131-page opinion the judge stated that because of cultural and racial bias IQ tests cannot be used as a valid measure of intellectual retardation for Blacks, and that Black children had been disproportionately assigned to inferior and dead-end education as a result of invalid assessments. The judge went on to state that even if there were in fact a 15 percent higher incidence of mental retardation in Black children, there would still be less than one chance in a million that a colorblind system could have produced the situation reported in the 1972 statistics, which showed that in California Blacks made up 9.3 percent of the total student population statewide and 25 percent of its mentally retarded classes.

Judge Peckham's permanent ban on using IQ tests to place Black children in mentally retarded classes in the state of California is a major forward step in the direction of protecting Black children from the abuses of intelligence testing. What needs to be brought into question in this discussion is the degree to which American psychologists have been involved in the enterprise of talent assessment, as opposed to talent development. For the past seventy-five years American psychologists have been obsessed with measuring, defining, classifying, and predicting intelligence as some static, gene-carried entity. By setting up school classification systems with categories such as gifted, superior, average, low average, border line, and retarded on the basis of a set of intellectual assessment tools whose predictive validity is open to serious questions when it comes to forecasting future scholastic attainment and overall performance in life itself, psychologists have allowed themselves to become the gatekeepers of opportunity within the American educational system. The correlation mentioned earlier between intelligence test scores and grades of 0.50 is not sufficiently above the chance level to warrant denying young people educational opportunities at any stage of their development, nor is it sufficient to brand children with labels announcing that they don't have the "right stuff," labels that will follow them through their educational history.

There is evidence to suggest that much of what is measured by traditional intelligence tests and scholastic aptitude examinations in the way of problem-solving styles, language competencies, and mathematical skills is learned behavior (Hunt, 1961; Brunner, 1963). The time has come to shift the emphasis in psychology toward building learning and teaching structures that will help children develop their talents. All children come into this world with a wide range of learning potential, with the possible exception of those with massive, visible, congenital defects. What the children learn and how much of this potential is actualized depends on the kinds of learning environments children are exposed to as they move through the critical growth stages. Psychologists need to find out more about how learning takes place in a variety of social and cultural contexts—formal, informal, spontaneous, episodic, structured, and unstructured—and use this knowledge to develop a flexible series of teaching and learning paradigms to facilitate the development of a maximum range of competencies in all children.

INTELLIGENCE, TEACHER EXPECTATIONS, AND THE LEARNING PROCESS

Despite its critics, controversies, and court cases, the IQ testing industry is very much alive in American education today. As children pass through their years in the public schools, they are given a variety of tests to assess their intelligence, abilities, aptitudes, potential to learn, and educational achievement. This information, which is contained in the child's cumulative school record, is readily available to teachers. On the basis of how the child is classified on these intellectual assessments—superior, average, slow, and the like—teachers can and do set up corresponding expectations of what scholastic level the learner should be able to achieve. Teacher expectations once established seem to influence the course of learning by setting up a self-fulfilling prophesy.

The teacher is a major force in the life of a child. In the classroom role he or she has the power to influence in either a negative or positive direction the level of the child's scholastic performance. The relationship between teacher expectations derived from intelligence test scores and the child's subsequent classroom performance was very clearly demonstrated in a classic experiment reported by Rosenthal and Jacobson (1968) in *Pygmalion in the Classroom*. The title comes from George Bernard Shaw's play *Pygmalion* where Liza Doolittle explains how expectations can influence how a person is perceived and how one relates to others: "You see, really and truly, apart from things anyone can pick up [the dressing and proper way of speaking and so on] the difference between a lady and a flower girl is not how she behaves, but how she is *treated*. I shall always be a flower girl to Professor Higgins because he treats me as a flower girl, always will, but I know I can be a lady to you because you treat me like a lady and always will."[2]

Rosenthal and Jacobson, using a sample of children from an elementary school with a high proportion of economically disadvantaged minority children in the south of San Francisco Bay area, randomly divided the children into two groups called the spurters and nonspurters. One out of every five children in each of eighteen classrooms consisting of grades one through six was arbitrarily designed as spurters. Teachers were told that children randomly classified as spurters would show impressive gains in intellectual and academic growth during the school year. In order to sound impressive, the researchers informed teachers that the predictions about

[2]Shaw, Bernard. *Pygmalion.* London: Constable & Co., Ltd., 1912, p. 17. Reprinted by permission of The Society of Authors on behalf of the Bernard Shaw Estate.

impressive gains were based on an intelligence test called the Harvard Test of Inflective Acquisition. There was, of course, no such test; this was done merely to attempt to create the expectations. The children designated as spurters did in fact make impressive gains when measured half way through the school year and again at the end of the school year. On a standardized IQ test, Flanigan's test of general abilities, the spurters gained an average of 41 IQ points compared to 16 points for the nonspurters, a difference of 25 points. The effects were more pronounced with first and second graders. The younger minority children presumably were more responsive to positive expectations because they had not been in school long enough to build up a repetitive cycle of negative contacts with their teachers. Children designated as spurters were also more likely to be described as happy, curious, and having a good chance for success in the future. In reviewing the behavior of teachers, Rosenthal and Jacobson noted that the children classified as spurters were treated with greater affection, understanding, and special attention, which may have improved the child's self-confidence and motivation to learn.

Subsequent investigations and discussions have tried to pin down exactly how teachers arrive at judgments about the ability levels of their students and how they behave towards students in order to create the expected outcome (Rist, 1970, 1972; J. Smith, 1979). The general conclusion is that teachers form opinions about student's ability levels on the basis of information normally contained in the child's cumulative school records. Opinions are not only formed from IQ test data, but are also influenced by race and socioeconomic level. Needless to say, race and socioeconomic level are statistically correlated with IQ. If a student has a low IQ, is Black, and is from a low socioeconomic group, he or she is more likely to be viewed as not having a high probability of achieving classroom success, especially by white teachers. Once established, expectations are resistant to change. Teachers tend to spend much less time in positive classroom contact with students whom they expect to be poor learners. Conversely, economically advantaged students with high IQs are perceived as having considerable learning potential. Teachers seem to invest a greater amount of positive effort in the high IQ, economically advantaged students, effort expressed in the form of more frequent praise, attention, affectionate gestures, and assignments to classroom leadership roles (Rist, 1972). The quality of the interpersonal relationship between teacher and student, enhanced by the confidence and affirmation the teacher expresses in the course of their interaction, has a decisive impact on the student's academic and social growth.

Carl Rogers (1974), David Aspy (1972), and Aspy and Roebuck (1974) have developed a conceptual model and a research methodology to examine the psychological quality of interpersonal relationships between teacher and student in terms of positive regard, empathy, and congruence (defined as genuineness or realness). From their experience in human relationships as educators and psychotherapists, Rogers and Aspy concluded that teachers who are willing to prize their students, who are willing to try to understand the world as it appears from the child's frame of reference, and who are willing to be real and genuine human beings in their relationships with students are able to facilitate or set into motion a process that results in measurable affective and intellectual growth for students. In their research teachers who showed a comparatively high level of positive regard, empathy, and congruence, as measured by ratings of their classroom behavior, created in their relationships with students a psychological climate that was associated with significant growth in learning rates, achievement test scores, self-concept, cognitive problem-solving skills, improved attendance records, and fewer discipline problems.

Fortunately, empathy, positive regard, and genuineness are not fixed, gene-carried behaviors. These facilitative characteristics are learned behaviors that can be developed through exposure to encounter growth groups and other actualizing experiences. Teachers who became more open, caring, and understanding as a result of their experiences in guided growth groups demonstrated a higher level of facilitative behaviors in their subsequent interaction with students. The students responded to the growth in their teachers with improved learning rates, achievement test scores, self-concept, cognitive problem-solving skills; their attendance improved and they displayed fewer discipline problems.

The initial research samples described by Rogers and Aspy were composed of white students. Subsequently Aspy (1974) looked at the effects of these interpersonal facilitative conditions on Black students. Not only did Black children show the same growth in achievement, cognitive problem-solving skills, self-concept, learning rates, attendance, and behavior, but they also showed a gain of approximately ten points in their IQ scores.

To briefly summarize the conclusions of Rogers, Aspy, and Rosenthal and Jacobson, the psychological quality of the interpersonal relationship, the critical variable in the teacher-student dyad, is measurably influenced by the teacher's personal values and his or her expectations of how well or how poorly the student will perform. Unfortunately, when it comes to the match between white teachers and Black students, a number of historical and sociocultural factors at work in the backgrounds of white teachers prevent them from being able to create a psychological climate characterized by the facilitative conditions of genuineness, positive regard, and empathic understanding in their relationships with Black students.

First, there is the racism inherent in American society. It is difficult if not impossible for teachers who have grown up in the American society to escape being tainted by attitudes of Anglo cultural and racial superiority, and the concomitant image of Blacks as mentally inferior sambos, clowns, noble savages, and beasts. Attitudes of Black inferiority on the part of white teachers, whether explicit or implicit, prevent teachers from seeing the intellectual strengths in Black students. Teachers who cannot perceive the strengths in their students are not likely to be able to relate to their students effectively or to motivate them to maximize their learning potential in the classroom. Many humanitarian liberal white teachers, those who love and want to save all poor Black folks, attempt to shield Black students from failure by operating with a permanent set of lowered expectations. Shielding Black students from failure by imposing a permanent set of lowered expectations is only another way of communicating to them that they are not capable of achieving.

Second, Black students may not closely approximate the Anglo teacher's ideal of what a good student acts like, talks like, and walks like. Not only do they not have the requisite IQ scores for the ideal student, but they also may not be passive, conforming, and quiet. Cultural differences in the behavioral styles of white teachers and inner-city Black youth are a potential source of conflict. In a research study conducted some years ago, Gottlieb (1964) examined the perceptions of white and Black teachers regarding Black students by asking the teachers to rank a series of descriptive adjectives. White teachers categorized Black students as lazy, talkative, high-strung, and rebellious, Black teachers perceived Black youth as happy, energetic, cooperative, and ambitious, and both groups of teachers ranked the students high on fun-loving. The differences in these perceptions of white and Black teachers can be interpreted as a tendency on the part of white teachers to misjudge the behavior styles of Black youth, an example of Nobles's (1978) transubstantiation. In viewing their behavior through an outside cultural lens, white teachers experienced the energy, vitality, enthusiasm, outgoingness, spontaneity, and high activity level reflected in the behavior of Black youth as deviant, maladjusted behavior, indicative of being "high-strung" and rebellious.

Mary Harvey's (1980) research on low-income Black students supports Gottlieb's findings. In her study of teachers in eight elementary schools in Portland, Oregon, teachers described low-income students, and particularly Black students, as being disruptive, hyperactive, unable to sit still, and too mobile. Teachers perceived low-income students as less intellectually capable and more in need of behavioral management techniques to reduce the high incidence of discipline problems and compensate for cultural deprivation. Behavioral management in the classroom was accomplished by a highly structured curriculum, set classroom routines, strict rules for pupil conduct, and high levels of teacher directedness and control. Active behaviors, even when appropriate, were discouraged. Enthusiastically volunteering answers was discouraged while passive but inappropriate behaviors, such as being inattentive but quiet, were praised. The reverse was true with high-income students. Low-income children were being taught to be passive, quiet, teacher-dependent, and uncreative. High-income children, on the other hand, were being taught to be teacher-independent, expressive, and creative.

The final divisive factor in the relationship between Black students and white teachers is in the students' cultural background, which values human relationships, feelings, genuineness, and emotional closeness. If the children feel that the teachers are devaluating them, do not like them, and do not consider them to be capable human beings, they are not likely to put forth their best efforts in the classroom. The teacher's negative attitude, no matter how well it is masked by the cloak of professionalism, sets into motion a chain of events that can elicit openly antagonistic, defiant, and withdrawal behaviors in children and these behaviors are then classified as adjustment problems.

The issues raised in this section, which began with the relationship between intelligence test scores and learning, suggest that we must take into consideration the teacher's attitudes, beliefs, expectations, and values about the academic strengths of Black children. If the teacher believes that Black children lack the capacity to learn, based on IQ scores, socioeconomic status, race, Anglo superiority, or cultural misunderstandings of the child's behavior, it is this belief rather than any gene-carried intellectual ability that has a powerful unfavorable influence on the teacher-student relationship and that ultimately undermines the student's academic progress. Teachers need help in looking at how their beliefs, values, and behavioral styles affect children. Training programs that take teachers beyond superficial intellectual discussions about cultural differences, racial relationships, and Black history are necessary. Teachers need to take a deeper look at themselves as persons, how they come across, how they judge and value others, how children perceive them, and most important, how these human characteristics affect the development of Black children. Looking at oneself is often painful, and the process of personal change is even more painful; however, if teachers are to build more constructive relationships with Black youth, it may be necessary for them to encounter and work through these growing pains.

ACHIEVEMENT MOTIVATION AND PSYCHOSOCIAL REALITY

Achievement motivation—the personal commitment to a standard of excellence, the willingness to persist in the challenge, struggle, excitement, and disappointment intrinsic in the learning process— is considered to have a major influence on academic performance, scholastic attainment, and success in life's major undertakings

(McClelland et al., 1953; Atkinson, 1966). In the achievement motivation hypothesis, school is conceived in terms of a meritocracy, analogous to the open marketplace, where each child has the opportunity to rise to the top of their educational attainment ladder. Children who are determined to develop their talents through hard work, persistence, and competitive struggle will excel in the school situation; children with an equivalent talent profile who are low in the personality traits associated with achievement motivation are not expected to do as well.

Achievement motivation is not only used to account for the differences in performance levels of children in the school situation but is also put forth to explain the accomplishments of the American people. America has been labeled the *Achieving Society* (McClelland, 1961), a country where the values of persistence in the face of obstacles, competition, commitment to a standard of excellence, future planning, and hard steady work over a prolonged period foster individual and group success. The achievement orientation has pushed this nation ahead as a world power in science, industry, technology, finance, and military might.

Since Black children do not perform academically as well as white children in school and, subsequently, as Black adults do not occupy positions of wealth, power, and prestige relative to their numbers in American society—there are no Black Rockefellers, Du Ponts, Kennedys, or Reagans—the simple inference from the achievement motivation theory is that Black children lack the commitment to the values of persistence, the pursuit of excellence, future planning, and hard work. They are simply lazy, shiftless, or incapable of responding to the rigors, challenges, and joys of mental discipline. By explaining the educational performance deficiencies of Black children in terms of inadequate personality characteristics in the child, the achievement motivation hypothesis fails to take into consideration major differences in the psychosocial realities that Black and white children encounter in the process of growing up within American society.

White children, especially middle-class and upper-middle-class white children, have every reason to believe that accomplishments in school will pay off in later life. The payoff will come in terms of opportunities for marriage, occupational choices, additional educational preparation, and entry into the professions. While there has been much debate about the exact relationship between educational attainment and success in later life (Jencks, 1972), there is no denial that educational training provides the person with the opportunity to enter a given professional, occupational, or advanced educational arena. It goes without saying that once people have satisfied the educational and training requirements to become brick layers, bakers, or physicians, there is a wide variance in their future economic and occupational success.

In addition to the idea of education as a pathway to future advancement that is being reinforced and encouraged by parents, teachers, and the society, white children also have concrete role models available to them from previous generations who have successfully followed the opportunity pathways provided by the educational system. The schooling and training backgrounds of the white community's skilled artisans, professionals, business executives, professors, health care workers, and TV news reporters represent visible evidence that the educational contract will be honored.

White youngsters learn very quickly as they move along the educational conveyor belt to value the external symbols of progress indicated by grades, proficiency reports, and test scores. These symbols are rewarded by parents, sometimes envied by other children, and can be cashed in like an investment with interest at some time in the future to gain admission to advanced elementary and high school programs, prestigious colleges, skilled training programs. They are valuable for meeting the right prospective marriage partners and essential for getting over the last big hurdle, admission to graduate and professional schools. The child is told repeatedly that grades are the meal ticket to the next level of choices. Young people become so obsessed with grades as the key to the future that they will literally cheat, lie, and steal copies of their professor's exams in order to achieve acceptable grades.

The classroom learning environments in America's public schools, where mandatory attendance laws turn the youngsters into a captive audience from early childhood to late adolescence, have been described by many observers as dull, repetitive, unstimulating, meaningless, and lacking in any coherent purpose as far as the student is concerned (Silberman, 1970). Children who enter school with the natural fascination, eagerness, and excitement to approach the joys and complexities of learning are quickly turned off in spite of periodic educational reforms such as open classrooms, child-centered learning, values clarification, competency-based learning, and multicultural education. In an educational environment where students are prevented from experiencing the excitement, struggle, and challenge of sequential discovery, it is no wonder that students become obsessed with grades, points on tests, and exam curves. Children submit to this dehumanization process not because of any internalized personal commitment to a standard of excellence, but because they see education as a ticket to future choices. By compelling students to submit, or at least making it attractive with secondary rewards for them to conform, do what they are told, memorize dull material, turn in repetitious assignments on time, hide their genuine feelings of confusion and disappointment, and compete with each other for extrinsic rewards and future payoffs, educators, albeit somewhat dishonestly and deceptively, are shaping a set of behaviors in children that will make them more acceptable to the corporate structure. They will be acceptable to the corporate structure to the degree that they will have internalized the values of the educational system reflected in the ethic of conformity, suppression of feelings and genuineness, compulsive time management, competition with others under the guise of cooperation, and an inability to experience the present fully because of constant worry about the future.

Black children refuse to submit to this educational dehumanization process. Black children do not believe that conformity to white values involving language, time management, future orientation, competition, deceptiveness, and suppression of spontaneity will guarantee them a reasonable chance for a job with a built-in growth ladder in the future. From their perspective, it doesn't make sense to spend years of concentrated effort on the sterile, dull, meaningless content of what passes for education in the typical American classroom when there is little assurance of a payoff at the end.

Black children see unemployed and underemployed high school, trade school, and even college graduates every day throughout the Black community. White children on the other hand, see people like themselves positioned in every visible area of employment, status, and decision making in the society. Concerned parents, teachers, coaches, ministers and other interested adults can tell Black children that things are changing for the better; they may try to make them aware of special programs specifically designed to train minority youth for skilled jobs or admit them to college, but no amount of convincing can mask the reality that there is not an equivalent range of opportunities for Black youth in America today. Black children are very perceptive (Baldwin, 1955). As they age, they become more aware of how maliciously white America has treated Black folks. The awareness of the historical legacy of racism does very little to encourage Black youth to trust the white's word about how things are changing and that the entry pathway into the world of expanding opportunity for Black youth is through education. The Black child is not deficient in motivation to struggle to grow, to excel, and to achieve; the deficiency is in the structure of institutional racism built into the fabric of American society. The psychosocial reality of oppression, based on an abundance of concrete evidence, is what prevents Black children from feeling realistically confident that by putting forth a sufficient amount of effort they have a solid chance of achieving a wide range of options.

Admittedly, the school as one institution cannot by itself change the structure of institutional racism in American society or the priorities of the government, the corporate system, labor unions, and the military in order to provide a greater range of opportunities for Black youth. This does not mean, however, that educators are powerless. Educators as a group are like sleeping giants who are only beginning to recognize what a potentially powerful force they can become within American society. During the past ten years, activist teacher unions have coalesced the power base of educators to provide substantive changes in such teacher-oriented issues as pay, fringe benefits, working conditions, classroom size, and teacher representation in matters of governance and in educational policy decisions (Corwin, 1974). Teacher organizations have endorsed political candidates, hired lobbyists, taken positions on legislative and funding issues, and contributed financially to political causes. This same power base could be used to combat institutional racism in American society by encouraging, pressuring, and even leaning on the corporate system, government, industry, colleges, and job-controlling institutions to give Black youth a wider access to viable opportunity networks.

Informal networks and person-to-person information banks play an important role in acquainting white youngsters with occupational role models and future educational choices. White children are exposed to informational networks and data banks through social clubs, athletic groups, family contacts, travel experiences, labor union summer activities, and a host of other youth programs sponsored conjointly by civic organizations, industry, and booster groups. In face-to-face encounters they can meet, question, interact with, and explore possible areas of interest with people who are already working and training to work in many different occupations. These periodic, incidental learning experiences provide white youth with more concrete ideas and contacts with respect to future work and educational opportunities than they usually get in their infrequent sessions with busy, overworked vocational counselors.

Black youth, especially those from low-income families, who are interested in the skilled trades, managerial positions, business careers, and the professions are often first-generation occupational pioneers. As such, Black youth seldom have the opportunity to actually meet, relate to, and be exposed to people who are working in various occupational capacities. They only rarely find out what they went through to get there and how to keep in touch with them. They have only a vague notion about the preparational steps involved in getting from where they are to where they might want to go. Educators can be instrumental in filling this gap between where Black youth are and where they might want to go by taking the leadership in encouraging the community power brokers and opinion molders to saturate the Black community with activities for youth that connect into mainstream-oriented person-to-person data banks and information networks. There are also Black-oriented person-to-person information banks and networks supported by civic groups, fraternal orders, sororities, political caucuses, small-business groups, and churches in the Black community. Career guidance counselors need to tune in to the Black community's grapevine, find out what's going on, and build a connecting link using the oral tradition between Black civic groups and the students.

For Black youth the advantage of being connected to Black-oriented networks is their greater exposure to Black role models. Black youth might find it easier to talk to another brother or sister, and it is definitely reassuring for the youth to see members of the Black community—even if they don't still live in the neighborhood—who are making it in the work world.

The greatest resource educators have available to them in their attempts to build bridges between Black youth and the work world of future achievement is the youth themselves. Outside of school Black youth are creatively struggling with the challenges of life by learning how to survive, how to be resourceful, how to take on responsibility within the extended family, how to cope with oppression, and how to integrate the duality of values represented in the Afro-American–Euro-American life styles. Educators should allow the classroom to be used as a forum for youth to discuss these critical issues, exchange problem-solving strategies, and develop alternatives. By providing the opportunity to confront survival and identity questions within the classroom, educators can tap into the energy, inventiveness, curiosity, and resourcefulness Black youth express outside of school in order to teach the opportunity-seizing skills Black youth need to make it in the mainstream economy and to help them establish a sense of purpose and direction for the future. Encouraging Black youth to discuss issues that are essential to their existence would definitely create some interest, involvement, and excitement in an otherwise dull classroom situation, an interest and excitement that might carry over into academic subjects once the students have developed a clear idea of what they are trying to accomplish.

LANGUAGE, COMMUNICATION, AND LEARNING

The communication of ideas and information between teacher and student by means of the spoken word is an essential ingredient of the learning process. Education has been described as a conversation between teacher and learner. Clarity and understanding in the communication of ideas between teacher and student by means of the spoken language is facilitated when both members of the communication unit are using an identical, or at least, a comparable, language system. Anyone who has listened to and compared the speech of inner-city Black children and their teachers will readily conclude that they are not using the same version of the English language. Sentences like "I ax John, do he be playin' basketball?" or "The poll-ice be comin' to the skatin' rink" characterize the language of Black students. The teacher, using standard oral English, would be more likely to say, "I asked John if he plays (is playing, will be playing, is usually playing) basketball," or "The police will be coming (are always coming, usually come) to the skating rink." The speech dialect that Black children use, sometimes called Black speech, Black English, and Black Language, obviously differs from what the teacher expects in terms of standard oral English. Black speech has been labeled by educators as substandard English, bad grammar, and slovenly, corrupt, disordered speech. Children who use Black speech in the classroom have been accused of having clumsy and lazy tongues.

The habitual use of substandard, disordered speech is considered to be responsible for learning disabilities in Black children because it prevents them from being able to understand verbal concepts and to express themselves correctly and clearly. Children who persist in utilizing Black speech in the classroom will find themselves being constantly corrected and encouraged to improve their pronunciation and grammer until their speech more closely resembles that of the teacher. The emphasis in the corrective-replacement approach is to empty out the disordered, substandard Black speech and replace it with acceptable, conventional standard oral English.

Black children respond to these constant attempts on the part of teachers to censure and correct their speech with at least four observable patterns of language behavior: blatant defiance, withdrawal, superconformity, and code switching. By the time children enter elementary and junior high school, their normal pattern of language usage has become a part of who they are as persons. Attacks on their language, however well-meaning, creates in some youngsters a pattern of resistance that can be expressed by either active defiance or withdrawal. The linguistically defiant Black child seems to take pride in the usage of Black speech and deliberately refuses to talk like white folks. The more the teacher tries to correct the child, the more the child refuses to conform verbally. The child and the teacher are locked into open verbal combat, with the child refusing to give an inch as indicated in comments to the teacher like: "I'm not going to say my mother is leaving bitch, when I say she be leavin' I means she be leavin'." Defiant behavior can get the child labeled as a behavioral problem with associated linguistic handicaps, followed up by referral to the school psychologist and/or speech pathologist.

Linguistically withdrawn children may feel intimidated by the teacher's censure of their language. Furthermore, when they try to speak they tend to experience conflict between two competing language systems, a kind of interference modification that reflects itself in stammering and stuttering. The late Jesse Owens, an outstanding track star who won three gold medals as a Olympic sprinter in 1936, was apparently very linguistically withdrawn as a child. After moving to Ohio from the deep South as an elementary school pupil, he was afraid to speak in school because of problems with stammering. The name Jesse comes from an aborted attempt on the part of Owens as a shy child to tell the teacher his name was J. C., which came out sounding like Jesse. Other children sometimes make fun of the stammering and stuttering caused by interference modification, which makes the withdrawn child even more hesitant to speak. Extremely withdrawn children, who stammer and stutter when they speak, run the risk of being classified as either autistic or nonverbal cripples, classifications that suggest the presence of a serious psychological disorder.

The superconforming youngsters completely internalize the speech of their teachers. For one reason or another, they decide to adopt standard oral English exclusively and completely reject any semblance of Black speech. These children may even go so far as attempting to correct the speech of their parents, other extended family members, peers, and people in the neighborhood. Emulating the corrective approach of their teachers with other Black folks may not make these little Lord Fauntleroys very popular in the community. Correcting people's speech can be dangerous, the person being corrected might interpret the corrective action as the wrong kind of signifying and "whoop" (whip) the little Black Lord Fauntleroy's ass.

The youngster who learns to switch codes develops a high level of fluency in both standard oral English and Black English. He feels comfortable using either language system and can shift easily from one to the other. These youngsters recognize that there are different language universes as represented by the home, school, and the streets. They seem to have an intuitive feel for the diversity of language and know how to fit their language to the social situation and language background of the listener. Many Black professionals developed considerable skill in code switching as children and young adults. They know how to get across using mainstream dialects to communicate when they are making a living interacting with Euro-Americans in their roles as physicians, psychotherapists, teachers, TV news announcers, and flight attendants. Some of their Euro-American colleagues would really be surprised to see how they talk when they are gettin' down in an all Black gathering.

As Black educators, sociolinguists, and psychologists became more influential in educational circles in the late 1960s and early 1970s, they challenged the conception of Black speech as bad grammar, substandard English, slovenly speech, lazy tongues, and clumsy lips. They questioned the soundness of language teaching methods based on the corrective-replacement approach. At a conference on the cognitive and language development of the Black child in 1973, the coined the term "Ebonics" (Black sounds), from a combination of the words Ebony and phonetics, as an all-encompassing label for linguistic and paralinguistic features of the verbal and nonverbal sounds, cues, and gestures that are systematically and predictably used in the process of communication by Afro-Americans (E. Smith, 1974; Williams, 1975b). Black educators, psychologists, and sociolinguists conceive of Black speech as part of a legitimate, alternate language system, similar in the deep structure to West African languages, with its own rules for syntax and pronunciation (Smitherman, 1977). The rules for Black speech involve contractions of the "ing" sounds: *walkin* versus *walking*; front shifting with primary stress on the first syllable: *poll-ice* versus *police*; a zero copula or different tense usage for the verb *to be*: *he busy, John playin* versus *he is busy, John is (*or *was) playing* (Williamson, 1975). Other features found in Black speech and described by Williamson include phonological contrast, r-less-ness, and simplification of final consonant clusters as described in Table 5–1.

Black youngsters can be thought of as having been exposed to two different versions of the English language, each with its own descriptive rules. Rather than trying to eradicate the Black version of the language completely, Black educators and sociolinguists encourage teachers to think of the child as potentially bilingual and to incorporate within the curriculum a strategy of language learning that incorporates the Black dialect as a foundation for building mainstream language skills.

The rationale for Black English as a legitimate alternative dialect with its own descriptive rules for grammar and pronunciation was supported in a decision rendered by United States Judge Charles Joiner on July 12, 1979, in Michigan Eastern District Court. In the case of *Martin Luther King, Jr., Elementary School Children* V. *Ann Arbor Michigan School Board,* the parents of a group of low-income Black students argued that their children were being denied an equal opportunity to education because of a language barrier that was preventing the children from learning how to read. The parents claimed that the teachers regarded Black English as sloppy speech, and scolded their children for using it; the parents de-

TABLE 5–1

PRONUNCIATION FEATURES IN
BLACK ENGLISH

1. Phonological contrast in *our* and *or* words	four = foe hoarse = horse
2. Deletion of final and middle *r*	paris = pass during = doing star = stah Carol = Cal
3. Simplification of final consonant clusters.	cold = col, cole toll = toe left = lef test = tes

Adapted from J. Williamson, "A Look at Black English," originally published in the August 1971, issue of *The Crisis*. Reprinted by permission.

manded that school authorities recognized Black English as a formal dialect with historical roots and grammatical rules of its own. Judge Joiner ruled, in what may become a precedent for future cases, that Black English is a distinct dialect, not corrupt speech, and directed the school district to prepare a plan to assist teachers in developing a better understanding of Black language and in learning how to teach reading to children who use Black speech (Kernan, 1979).

The Black community is not in complete agreement about the utilization of Black speech in the formal classroom setting. Carl Rowan, a noted newspaper columnist, and Kenneth Clark, a well-known Black psychologist, reject the bilingual analogy. They are of the opinion that using Black speech as part of a strategy to teach standard English only reinforces the use of nonstandard speech, slows Black children down, and prevents them from developing the conventional language skills they will need to succeed in the mainstream (Kernan, 1979; Sheils, 1976).

In order to comprehend fully the importance of Ebonics in the psychosocial world of the Black child, it is necessary to examine the relationship between the sociocultural dynamics of language and the way the child interacts with others, learns, and conceptualizes. The spoken word is the most powerful force in the Black experiential, phenomenal field. Language extends beyond grammar and pronunciation. The Black heritage, cultural identity, and psychological perspective are transmitted through the oral tradition. The spoken word is the unifying force through which all human experiences in the Black community intersect (Smitherman, 1977). Expressive speech is a performance on the stage of life (Holt, 1975). The Black youngster learns to interact with others, express feelings, filter information, and understand conceptual relationships by means of the spoken word. Skill with the spoken word, the ability to "run it down" and to "talk that talk" is part of one's identity. A youngster is known by his or her rap. The rap becomes part of the youngster's reputation (Smitherman, 1977). A "bad rap" will get you over, help you achieve your goals in social situations, and is most definitely necessary if a brother "be wantin' to rhapsodize the ladies." The participatory, innovative, affective, and conceptual aspects of Ebonics are a vital part of the experience base the child brings to the school situation.

The participatory component of Black language involves a high level of simultaneous verbal and nonverbal interaction between speaker and listener. The speaker sends out words and the listener signals encouragement, understanding, agreement, acknowledgement, or disagreement by actively responding to the speaker while the speaker is still talking. These signals from the listener to the speaker come in a variety of "oh yeah's" "right on's," "ooo-eee's," and "I can dig its." This call–response dialogue is further amplified as either the speaker or the listener reach out and literally touch each other during the conversation with Black handshakes, "gimme fives" and other nonverbal cues such as eye rolling and head nodding (Cooke, 1980). Black children go through their preschool and outside school learning experiences and social interaction using this participatory language.

The spoken word in the classroom is expressed in a much more structured and controlled manner. Children are expected to wait until they are properly acknowledged before responding to ideas expressed by the teacher and by other students. Spontaneous participation is not encouraged. Children are admonished to be quiet and to exercise self-control so that the learning can take place. Apparently the noise of the children enthusiastically volunteering to answer questions and interacting with each other distracts the teacher and makes it impossible for him or her to concentrate on teaching. If the children persist in any sort of call-response behavior, they are likely to get themselves classified as talkative, disruptive, and lacking in self-control.

Outside the classroom, the Black child is learning to use words in a very imaginative, figurative, and colorful fashion. In order to capture attention and generate response from their peers, children are expected to enrich the reality they are trying to describe with idioms, analogies, metaphors, and comparisons that can be understood from the collective experience base of the listeners. Inside the classroom the child is being taught to use words to describe and replay events in a literal, verbatim matter. Rather than describing a sequence of events involving a fight between two youngsters with statements to the effect that "John was angry with Jim, a fight ensued, and Jim appeared to get the worst of it," a Black youngster is likely to say, "John was mad as a big dog (probably because he lost the game of the dozens), and he pitched a boogie upside Jim's head, turned him every way but loose." The youngster can innovatively describe, define, and control the reality being experienced by processing words and phrases through an Afro-American cultural-linguistic filter. Through this ethnotropic[3] filtering Black youngsters can project reality in a way that capitalizes on the strengths of Black folks. Negative labels can be turned around so that brothers and sisters referred to as having "clumsy lips" and speaking "bad English" are actually being described as articulate speakers.

The expressive language that Black youth are learning to use in the community is rich in feeling. Life is given to ideas by generating ethnotropisms that suggest visual images of intensity: conversing with a handsome young woman is expressed as "firing on a stone fox"; reorganizing one's life space is described as "laying on the cut until I'm wired up"; a fancy car or motorcycle is a "hog"; drinking too much is known as "gettin' one's head raggedy," or being "higher than nine kites on a breezy day." Ideas and information are communicated with excitement and enthusiasm, feelings are not detached from ideas. As children progress through school, they are taught to focus more and more on the purely cognitive properties of ideas. In keeping with the Euro-American values, ideas are sterilized to provide the appearance of objectivity and scientific detachment. Excitement, enthusiasm, and vividness are discouraged because they might suggest that the speaker is too involved or—God forbid—too emotional.

A major dimension of this Black figurative speech is the propensity to describe events in terms of likenesses, similarities, and analogies. The Black child thinks not of a world in which entities are independent and separate, but of a world in which things are related. The child can visualize and creatively synthesize their common properties. A boy is not described as being merely being a fast runner but is depicted as being able to "move faster than four bloods in tennis shoes," who at the beginning of the race came out "smokin' like a big-ass jet." In the epic poem "Shine and The Great Titanic," the sharks in the water are not merely waiting for Shine to dive into the water, but the "sharks in the water are *singing* Shine o Shine

---

[3]Ethnotropism is the use of a word, phrase, or utterance in a different cultural context for the purpose of giving life or emphasis to an idea.

bring your Black ass to me." A person doing well in a particular activity is said to be "gettin' over like a fat rat in a cheese factory." The ability to use metaphors and analogies, to be able to think in terms of comparative visual images, and the use of presentational symbols to describe abstract relationships is a conceptual style that is generally thought to represent an advanced stage of language, communicative competence, and thought development (Holt, 1975; Piaget, 1970). In the linguistic socialization process of the Afro-American community, the Black child becomes adept in the use of these advanced forms of language, suggesting a high level of conceptual mastery and advanced communicative competence. This figurative, symbolic, ethnotropic, linguistic style is not reinforced by the normal elementary and junior high school language arts curriculum with its focus on correct grammar, pronunciation, and word usage confined to exact literal meanings defined within a Euro-American context. Black children learn words in school they cannot translate into the style of Ebonics; in school they are not allowed to use the Black linguistic style they are most familiar with. The end product of this split cultural phenomenon is often a student who can dazzle his or her peers with words outside of school while in the classroom he or she is perceived as a verbally destitute, slow learner.

Incorporating the participatory, innovative, metaphoric, and affective features of Black language into the classroom would allow children to use existing expressive and conceptual skills as a foundation for strengthening and expanding their language competencies. This can be done by developing language exercises that build a bridge between Black language styles and the traditional language skills the school is trying to teach.

The need to use language in innovative and creative ways can be tapped by allowing children to express the same story in a variety of ways, street talk, home talk, school talk, and TV-announcer English, and the like. Gary Simpkins (1977) attempts to accomplish this in a bridging program where he begins the reading program for high school Black youth using neighborhood expressive patterns and progresses in successive approximations to standard oral English. An example of Simpkins reading program appears in Table 5–2.

TABLE 5–2

LANGUAGE BRIDGING–
READING EXERCISE

Black English	Transition Form	Standard English
No matter what neighborhood you be in . . . young dudes gonna be having they wheels . . . You know how brothers be with they wheels. They definitely be keeping them clean, clean, clean.	No matter what neighborhood you look in . . . if you find teenagers, you'll find old cars. . . . Most teenagers can't afford a new or late model car. But they can . . . buy an old car. They lose they cars. They spend most of their time taking care of them.	Young people, Black or white, love their cars. They must have a car, no matter how old it is. James Russell was a young man who loved his car . . . '59 Chevrolet. He spent a great deal of time keeping his car clean. He was always washing and waxing it.

Adapted from G. Simpkins et al., *Bridge: A Cross-Cultural Reading Program* (Boston: Houghton Mifflin, 1977). Reprinted by permission.

Another variation of the bridging concept is to allow children themselves to create translations from old English to standard oral English to Black English, which might come out something like the sequence presented in Table 5–3.

Listening and expressive exercises that teach students to comprehend and express the same ideas in different language formats provide them with experiences in the diversity of language. Exposure to the rich diversity in language usage enables children to learn that there are no absolute prescriptive rules for language. Ideas can be expressed clearly using a variety of linguistic styles, the proviso being that if the speaker wants to be understood, it is essential to consider the background of the listener and the social setting.

Embedded in the controversy concerning the proper place of Black language and culture in the classroom learning situation are fundamental questions relating to the role of feelings in education and questions that involve differences between Euro-Americans and Afro-Americans in the development of conceptual styles.

TABLE 5–3

LANGUAGE BRIDGING

OLD ENGLISH–STANDARD ENGLISH–BLACK ENGLISH

Old English—Shakespeare	Standard English	Black English
Alas! Poor Yorick. I knew him, Horatio; a fellow of infinite jest of most excellent fancy; he hath borne me on his back a thousand times; and now, how abhorred in my imagination it is!	Poor Yorick! I really knew him Horatio—a man of great good humor. Of fantastic imagination; he helped me through many hard times, and I feel just terrible about this.	My Man Yorick! We was real tight, Horatio, I mean. The dude be crazy but he saved my ass many times. What you think, man? It really took me out.

It would be much easier to get youngsters turned on to the learning process in all areas if educators could capture the essence of the excitement, spontaneity, and drama that characterizes the language of Black children outside the classroom. The structure of formal education with its emphasis on regimentation, order, control, and above all else, being quiet seems to be deliberately geared toward preventing youngsters from sharing feelings of excitement, curiosity, anger, sadness, and enchantment. Learning as defined by the school is apparently supposed to be ascetic intellectual work, devoid of feelings. Many Black youngsters are turned off by the lifeless, sterile atmosphere of their classrooms. Gary Simpkins (1972) in an essay, "The Black Six-Hour Retarded Child" describes how the turned-off behavior of Black youngsters is misdiagnosed by their teachers. During the six hours of the school day the youngsters are perceived by their teachers as sullen, withdrawn, verbally deficient slow learners, children who are unable or unwilling to participate in the learning activity. Educators view this unproductive classroom behavior as indicative of severe retardation, behavior disorders, and psychological disturbances, as opposed to questioning whether it could be the constrictive structure of the learning situation that is creating this unresponsive behavior in Black youngsters. After school, however, these same youngsters become very much alive, mentally alert, and resourceful in terms of interacting with their peers, using innovative language, playing the dozens, finger popping, signifying, and rapping on the little foxes.

Carl Rogers (1974), one of America's preeminent psychologist-educators, has consistently expressed the view that education should incorporate both feelings and ideas. Children are not just intellectual creatures, they also feel love and hurt. Bringing together both feelings and ideas in the learning setting allows children the opportunity to begin to integrate and balance the affective and cognitive aspects of themselves as human beings. The absence of an affective dimension in the curriculum robs children of the excitement, thrill, and romance involved in discovering the beauty of ideas, the elegance of logical systems, and the grace of mathematical equations. The excitement, thrill, and romance children feel when they are beginning to understand the rudimentary outlines of a complex idea can serve as a motivating force to sustain them through the slow, tedious, sometimes frustrating period it takes to achieve technical precision and to move from precision to an understanding of how the general principles involved in the subject matter fit together and can be related to other areas of learning. The conception of learning as a progression from romance to precision to generalization comes from Whitehead (1929). Athletic coaches and marching band teachers seem to have an intuitive feel for learning that involves romance, precision, and generalization. Black kids who have for one reason or another felt the enchantment of athletics or of music will go over the same drill hour after hour, day after day. The precise mastery of the fundamentals involved in these drills not only teaches persistence, self-confidence, and discipline, but through these activities youngsters develop a deeper understanding of what music and sports are all about.

The conceptual style reflected in the metaphors, similes, analogies, and figures of speech of Black children emphasizes synthesis, correspondence, relationships, and likenesses. In school, children are taught to think in a Euro-American conceptual fashion with a primary focus of how things are different, separate, and distinct from each other. Students at all levels of Euro-American education gain considerable experience in breaking things down, reductionistic thinking, and on how to be severely critical. They often have very little awareness about how things fit together, especially in their educational experiences prior to graduate school. The element of synthetic thinking, which is already part of the linguistic repertory of Black children, needs to be introduced much earlier for all children to prevent them from being at a loss when it comes to putting these concepts together, identifying the big picture, and comprehending unifying principles. This is not to imply that children do not need to learn analytical thinking; analytical thinking is essential to understanding the unique properties of concepts and ideas. What is being proposed is that children be taught to conceptualize in a three-dimensional mode of thesis, antithesis, and synthesis.

THE ADDITIVE NATURE OF LEARNING

The recurring theme throughout this chapter and in the previous recommendations for using the child's existing language and conceptual skills as a bases for further learning was the additive principle of learning. Children can master new material very quickly when the teacher uses the child's existing experience pool, both affectively and cognitively, as a foundation on which to build new learning experiences. According to the Greeks, it is the culture that educates; the experience of life itself is a learning tree (Parks, 1963). The Black child who has been exposed to the Afro-American culture brings to the school environment a sense of emotional vitality and resilience, survival skills, suspicions about the future, and a style of communicating, interacting with others, processing information, and synthesizing his or her thoughts. Educators seem unable to utilize the Black child's Afro-American experience base effectively as a foundation for building additional competencies, skills, and mastery functions. The Black child's existing areas of mastery, skills, and potential for the future are not accurately assessed by traditional intelligence, aptitude, and achievement tests. Legitimate cultural differences are not sufficiently acknowledged, and the child's behavior, language, and affective and cognitive styles tend to be misperceived. The more the child fails to approximate the teacher's ideal of a child who is white, middle-class, does what he is told, contains his or her feelings, speaks in TV-announcer English, believes what the teacher says, and has few doubts about the relationship between school performance and future payoffs, the more likely the child will be judged as having deficits in ability, motivation, and self-control. Teachers get caught up in a corrective course of action designed to replace the unacceptable behavior with behaviors that more closely approximate their expectations of the mythical ideal child. Children react to this censure with anger, resentment, and withdrawal. The end result is a collision of cultural styles in the classroom that seems to lock Black children and their teachers in a power struggle that neither side fully understands. In the context of this clash of life styles it is difficult for the teacher and the student to establish the kind of productive, working interpersonal relationship that is a major facilitative condition for meaningful education (Rogers, 1974). As the struggle between Black students and their teachers continues, the students fall further and further behind in measurements of educational progress, which, ironically, confirms hypotheses about their being intellectually deficient, culturally deprived, and genetically inferior.

The cultural collision between educators and Black students will not be resolved by further victim analysis studies. Putting the blame on Black children shields educators from looking at themselves and how they can participate more constructively in the growth of Black students. A sound educational policy built on a foundation of additive learning must bring into play the experience base the Black child brings to school. In order to bring the Black experience base into a more prominent role in the educational milieu, teachers need a greater exposure to the heritage, cultural dynamics, life styles, relationship patterns, developmental stages, and psychological characteristics of Afro-Americans. Multicultural education is a step in the right direction, but too often this approach ends up being a superficial gimmick designed to keep the community quiet and to serve as a compensatory or remedial stop gap until Black children are ready for what educators regard as more serious education.

Preservice and in-service training for educators who are going to work with Black students should be geared toward three primary objectives: (1) developing instructional strategies, (2) building positive relationships between teachers and students, and (3) generating more responsive intellectual, cognitive, and achievement-assessment approaches.

The key to building more effective instructional strategies is to incorporate the phenomenal world of the child as it is reflected in the child's existing learning styles, language, conceptual patterns, ways of relating to others, and perceptions of the future. Children should see themselves as they are, the world as it appears to them, and what is important to them reflected in the curriculum. New skills can be developed using the child's existing experience base as a bridge. Equivalency of learning outcomes can be achieved by incorporating cultural diversity in teaching strategies.

Teachers cannot build relationships with Black students based on the facilitative conditions of empathy, congruence, and positive regard if they are unaware of what's happening in the student's world, feel uneasy when they are around them, and cannot identify strengths in their students. Didactic training in the Black heritage, life styles, and psychological perspectives can be used to increase the teacher's awareness of Afro-American psychological and sociocultural dynamics. To help teachers see how they are coming across in relationships with Black students and to evaluate the impact of instructional strategies, teachers can be provided with feedback from audio-visual recordings of actual and simulated teaching situations in guided growth groups along the lines suggested by Rogers (1974) and Aspy (1974).

Traditional IQ testing for Black children should be eliminated as much as possible. The history of past abuse and potential risk for future abuse is too great to permit the traditional IQ practices to continue. To the extent that tests of cognitive ability have to be employed, regardless of whether or not they are culturally free, culturally specific, or Blackanized, two protective considerations should be adopted as guidelines in selecting testing procedures. First, the testing methodology should be geared toward assessing how the child is progressing in terms of a clearly defined developmental scale of mental operations, beginning with sensory-motor concepts and progressing through preoperational concepts to an understanding of increasingly abstract number and verbal concepts, discriminant analysis, convergent and divergent thinking, symbol manipulation, and conservation (Barnes, 1973). For example, can the mental test provide us with a picture of how the child is progressing in terms of understanding concepts such as up–down, left–right, more than–less than, past–future, how objects are alike and different, and simple to complex number concepts? Second, can the testing procedure be regarded as meeting the criterion Asa Hilliard (1977) refers to as prescriptive validity? To meet the criterion of prescriptive validity, a set of specific guidelines or prescriptions for appropriate learning interventions must emerge from the results of the testing to teach the child the mental operations that have not yet been mastered. The results of the testing should generate a subsequent constructive developmental, rather than remedial, experience so that the child's educational growth can continue without damage to his or her self-image.

REFERENCES

Aspy, David. *Toward a Technology for Humanizing Education.* Champaign, Ill.: Research Press, 1972.

Aspy, David, and Roebuck, Flora. "From Humane Ideas to Human Technology and Back Again Many Times," *Education,* 95, no. 2 (1974), 163–171.

Atkinson, John. *A Theory of Achievement Motivation.* New York: John Wiley, 1966.

Aubry, Ernest L. "Larry P. vs. Wilson Riles—Erroneous Classification and Disproportionate Placement of Blacks in Classes for the Educable Mentally Retarded in California Public School Systems." Paper presented to the Southern California Association of Black Psychologists Workshop on Human Behavior and the Black Experience, Culver City, Calif. April 12, 1975.

Baldwin, James. *Notes of a Native Son.* New York: Bantam Books, 1955.

Barnes, Edward. "IQ Testing and Minority School Children: Imperatives for Change," *Journal of Non-White Concerns in Personnel and Guidance,* 2, no. 11, (1973), 4–20.

BLOCK, N. J., and DWORKIN, GERALD. *The IQ Controversy*. New York: Random House, 1976.

BINET, ALFRED, and SIMON, THEODORE. *The Development of Intelligence in Children*, trans. Elizabeth S. Kite. Baltimore: Williams & Wilkin, 1916.

BRIDGEMAN, B., and SHIPMAN, V. C. *Disadvantaged Children and Their First School Experience*. Report prepared for Project Head Start. Washington, D.C.: Office of Child Development, 1975.

BRUNNER, JEROME G. *The Process of Education*. New York: Random House, 1963.

CLARK, KENNETH. *Dark Ghettos: Dilemmas of Social Power*. New York: Harper & Row, 1965.

COLEMAN, JAMES, ET AL. *Equality of Educational Opportunity*. Washington, D.C.: U.S. Government Printing Office, 1966.

COOKE, BENJAMIN. "Non Verbal Communication Among Afro-Americans," pp. 139–160 in Reginald Jones, ed., *Black Psychology*. New York: Harper & Row, 1980.

CORWIN, RONALD. *Education in Crisis: A Sociological Analysis of Schools and Universities in Transition*. New York: John Wiley, 1974.

CRONBACH, LEE. *Essentials of Psychological Testing*. New York: Harper & Row, 1949.

DENTON, HERBERT. "Future Still Bleak for Black Children, Lobbying Group's Statistics Show," *Los Angeles Times*, January 14, 1981, Part 1A, p. 4

DEUTSCH, MARTIN, ed. *The Disadvantaged Child*. New York: Basic Books, 1967.

FINCHER, JACK. *Human Intelligence*. New York: Putnam's, 1976.

FINE, BENJAMIN. *The Stranglehold of the IQ*. New York: Doubleday, 1975.

FRANKLIN, VINCENT. "Black Social Scientists and the Mental Testing Movement, 1920–1940," in Reginald Jones, *Black Psychology*, (2nd ed.). New York: Harper & Row, 1980.

FOGELSON, R. M. *Los Angeles Riots*. New York: Arno Press, 1969.

GOTTLIEB, DAVID. "Teaching and Students: The Views of Negro and White Teachers," *Sociology of Education*, 37 (Summer 1964), 345–353.

GUTHRIE, ROBERT. *Even the Rat Was White: A Historical View of Psychology*. New York: Harper & Row, 1976.

HAGER, PHILLIP. "IQ Testing to Place Pupils in Retarded Classes Banned," *Los Angeles Times,* October 17, 1979, pp. 1–3.

HARLOW, HARRY; McGAUGH, JAMES; and THOMPSON, RICHARD. *Psychology.* San Francisco: Albion Publishing Co., 1971.

HARVEY, MARY. "The Public School Treatment of Low-Income Children: Education for Passivity," *Urban Education,* 15, no. 3 (October 1980), 279–324.

HELLMUTH, JEROME, ED. *Disadvantaged Child–Compensatory Education: A National Debate.* New York: Brunner/Mazel, 1970.

HILLIARD, ASA. "The Predictive Validity of Norm Referenced Standardized Tests: Piaget or Binet," *Negro Educational Review,* 28, no. 3, 4 (July and October 1977), 189–201.

HERRNSTEIN, RICHARD. "IQ," *Atlantic,* September 1971, pp. 43–64.

———. *IQ in the Meritocracy.* Boston: Little, Brown, 1973.

HOLT, GRACE. "Metaphor, Black Discourse Style, and Cultural Reality," in Robert L. Williams, ed, *Ebonics: The True Language of Black Folks.* St. Louis: Institute of Black Studies, 1975.

HUNT, J. McVICKER. *Intelligence and Experience.* New York: Ronald Press, 1961.

JENCKS, CHRISTOPHER, ET AL. *Inequality: A Reassessment of the Effect of Family Life and School in America.* New York: Basic Books, 1972.

JENSEN, ARTHUR. "How Much Can We Boost IQ and Scholastic Achievement?" *Harvard Educational Review,* 39, no. 1 (Winter 1969), 1–123.

———. *Bias in Mental Testing.* New York: Free Press, 1980.

KAMIN, LEON. *The Science and Politics of IQ.* New York: John Wiley, 1974.

KARIER, CLARENCE. "Testing for Order and Control in the Corporate Liberal State," in N. Block and G. Dworkin, eds., *The IQ Controversy.* New York: Random House, 1976.

KERNAN, MICHAEL. " 'Black English' Course Closely Studied," *Los Angeles Times,* October 24, 1979, Part 1A, pp. 7–8.

LANDECK, BEATRICE. *Learn to Read/Read to Learn: Poetry and Prose from Afro-Rooted Sources.* New York: D. McKay, 1975.

Larry P. et al. v. Wilson Riles. Civil Action No. C-71-2270, United States District Court, Northern California, San Francisco, Calif. 1972, 1979.

Martin Luther King Junior Elementary School Children et al. v. *Ann Arbor School District.* United States District Court, Eastern Michigan, Detroit, Mich. 1979.

McClelland, David. *The Achieving Society.* New York: Irvington Publishers, 1961.

McClelland, D. C.; Atkinson, J. W.; Clark, R. A.; and Lowell, E. L. *The Achievement Motive.* New York: Irvington Publishers, 1953.

Nobles, Wade. "Toward an Empirical and Theoretical Framework for Defining Black Families," *Journal of Marriage and the Family,* November 1978, pp. 679–688.

Owens, Jesse, with Paul G. Neimark. *The Jesse Owens Story.* New York: Putnam's, 1970.

Parks, Gordon. *The Learning Tree.* New York: Harper & Row, 1963.

Piaget, Jean. *The Science of Education and the Psychology of the Child.* New York: Orion, 1970.

Riessman, Frank. *The Culturally Deprived Child.* New York: Harper & Row, 1962.

Rist, Ray. "Student Social Class and Teacher Expectations: The Self Fulfilling Prophecy in Ghetto Education," *Harvard Educational Review,* 40, no. 3 (1970), 411–451.

———. "The Self-Fulfilling Prophecy in Ghetto Education," in J. McVicker Hunt, ed., *Human Intelligence.* New Brunswick, N.J.: Transaction Books, 1972.

Rogers, Carl. "Can Learning Encompass Both Ideas and Feelings?" *Education,* 95, no. 2 (1974), 103–114.

Rosenthal, Robert, and Jacobson, Lenore. *Pygmalion in the Classroom.* New York: Holt, Rinehart & Winston, 1968.

———. "Teacher Expectations for the Disadvantaged," *Scientific American,* April 1968, pp. 19–23.

Schrag, Peter. "End of the Impossible Dream," *Saturday Review,* September 19, 1970, pp. 68–70, 92–96.

Shaw, Bernard. *Pygmalion.* London: Constable Publishers, 1912.

Sheils, Merrill. "Why Johnny Can't Write," *Newsweek,* December 8, 1975, pp. 58–62, 65.

———. "Bridge Talk," *Newsweek,* December 20, 1976, pp. 68, 73.

Shockley, William. "Negro IQ Deficit: Failure of a 'Malicious

Coincidence' Model Warrants New Research Proposals," *Review of Educational Research*, 41 (1971), 227–48.

SILBERMAN, CHARLES. *Crisis in the Classroom*. New York: Random House, 1970.

SIMPKINS, GARY A.; GUNNING, THOMAS; AND KEARNY, ANNETTE. "The Black Six-Hour Retarded Child." *Journal of Non-White Concerns*, 2 (1973), 29–34.

SIMPKINS, GARY; HOLT, GRACE; AND SIMPKINS, CHARLESETTA. *Bridge: A Cross-Cultural Reading Program*. Boston: Houghton Mifflin, 1977.

SMITH, ERNIE. "Evolution and Continuing Presence of the African Oral Tradition in Black America." Doctoral Dissertation submitted to the University of California, Irvine, Fall 1974.

SMITH, JOAN. "Ascribed and Achieved Student Characteristics in Teacher Expectancy: Relationship of Socio-Economic Status to Academic Achievement, Academic Self Concept, and Vocational Aspirations." Doctoral Dissertation submitted to the University of Illinois, Chicago Circle, 1979.

SMITHERMAN, GENEVA. *Talkin and Testifyin: The Language of Black America*. Boston: Houghton Mifflin, 1977.

STODDARD, GEORGE. *The Meaning of Intelligence*. New York: Macmillan, 1943.

TERMAN, LEWIS. *The Measurement of Intelligence*. Boston: Houghton Mifflin, 1916.

———. *Intelligence Tests and School Reorganization*. New York: World Book Co., 1923.

———. "The Conservation of Talent," *School and Society*, 19, no. 483 (March 1924), 363.

TERMAN, LEWIS, and MERRILL, M. A. *Measuring Intelligence*. Boston: Houghton Mifflin, 1937.

THOMAS, CHARLES. "Psychology, Black Psychologists and the Legacy of Martin D. Jenkins." Paper presented to the Southern California Association of Black Psychologists Conference on Survival in the Black Community, Los Angeles, November 1979.

TUDDENHAM, R. D. "The Nature and Measurement of Intelligence," in L. Postman, ed., *Psychology in the Making*. New York: Knopf, 1962.

VOYAT, GILBERT. "IQ: God Given or Man Made?" *Saturday Review,* May 17, 1969, p. 52.

WHITEHEAD, ALFRED NORTH. *The Aims of Education.* New York: Macmillan, 1929.

WILLIAMS, ROBERT. "Bitch 100: A Culture-Specific Test." Paper presented to the American Psychological Association Convention, Honolulu, September 1972a.

———. "Bitch 100: A Culture-Specific Test," Williams and Associates, Inc., 6374 Delmar Blvd. St. Louis, Mo. 63130, 1972b.

———. "The Problem of Match and Mismatch," pp. 67–75 in L. Miller ed., *The Testing of Black Children.* Englewood Cliffs, N.J.: Prentice-Hall, 1974.

———. "Developing Cultural Specific Assessment Devices: An Empirical Rationale," in Robert Williams, ed., *Ebonics: The True Language of Black Folks.* St. Louis: Institute of Black Studies, 1975a.

WILLIAMS, ROBERT, ed. *Ebonics: The True Language of Black Folks.* St. Louis: Institute of Black Studies, 1975b.

WILLIAMSON, JUANITA. "A Look at Black English," pp. 11–21 in Robert Williams, ed., *Ebonics,* 1975.

CHAPTER SIX

MENTAL HEALTH AND THE BLACK COMMUNITY

THE REQUIREMENTS
FOR A MENTAL HEALTH
DELIVERY SYSTEM

It is essential for Black people to lay out the specifications for a community mental health agenda that meets the following three requirements: (1) defines mental health, psychological wellness, self-actualization, and growth-oriented counseling and psychotherapy from an Afro-American perspective; (2) identifies the barriers that prevent Blacks as a group from being able to develop to their fullest potential; (3) sets up operational strategies, goals, and objectives for mental health delivery systems.

Wade Nobels (1976), drawing on the thinking of Alfred Memmi (1965), states that for oppressed persons to be psychologically free, they must define themselves independent of the master. Whites in psychiatry, the behavioral sciences, and popular folklore (Thomas and Sillen, 1972) have traditionally defined Blacks in terms of inferiority, pathology, invisibility, and deprivation. The images of Afro-Americans created by the Euro-American deficit-deficiency hypothesis are not congruent with a philosophy of healthy psychological functioning, actualization, self-determination, and Black liberation. Furthermore, the Euro-American concept of mental health services for both Blacks and whites has its roots in a model of illness, insanity, abnormality, and psychological disorder. In the mental illness model, there is something wrong with the person who needs psychological services rather than with a society that creates psychological distress by fostering severe emotional repression, ruthless competition, dominance over others, narcissistic self-concern, and the relentless pursuit of power, and that perceives differences in terms of deviance. People who cry out for help with overt symptoms of emotional distress, despair, and alienation rather than suffer quiet lives of desperation and those who choose to be different run the risk of being diagnosed as psychologically abnormal. The corrective therapies associated with the mental illness model concentrate on straightening out the deficits within the person, controlling behavior by means of psychotropic drugs, and when all else fails, placing the person in a custodial environment.

The inclination to concentrate on repairing psychological defects and abnormality in the individual experiencing psychological distress has persisted despite the mandate of the Kennedy administration (1963) to seek out, eradicate, and prevent the causes of psychological misery. Neither *The Sane Society* (Fromm, 1955), "Camelot", nor Martin Luther King Jr.'s *Beloved Community* have emerged, and we are not yet saved.

Under the mental illness model Blacks historically tended to be diagnosed as having higher rates of the more severe forms of psychiatric disorders such as chronic schizophrenia, incipient paranoia, uncontrolled aggressive reactions, and impulse disorders (Thomas and Sillen, 1972; Block, 1980). Blacks have also been stereotyped in the psychiatric literature as not being psychologically minded, as lacking the psychological sophistication and motivation necessary for successful psychotherapy, as having a primitive character structure, and as being too jovial to be depressed and too impoverished to experience object loss (Adebimpe, 1981). This tendency to misdiagnose and overdiagnose severe psychopathology has persisted despite the awareness of sociocultural differences between Blacks and whites brought about by the Black revolution (L. King, 1978). In a recent study Adebimpe (1981) found that Black patients run a higher risk of being misdiagnosed as schizophrenics, whereas white patients showing identical behavior are more likely to be diagnosed as depressed. According to Adebimpe the errors in the diagnoses of Black patients can be accounted for by looking at the sociocultural distance between Black patients and white psychiatrists reflected in the vocabulary, modes of communication, dress style, value systems, and how distress and emotions are expressed. These sociocultural factors and societal values affect the psychiatrist's clinical impression of diagnostic signs and symptoms.

As a result of this history of misdiagnoses and stereotypes, prospective Black patients are reluctant to seek the help of psychiatrists, psychologists, and other licensed mental health professionals for assistance in resolving emotional conflicts. Black people view the psychiatrist's world as alien turf, tend not to seek help until the situation approaches a crisis (Sue, 1977; Block, 1980), and are correct in their assumption that they may be diagnosed as crazy, delusional, or psychotic if they open up and honestly run down what's bothering them, especially if their conflicts involve beliefs about events experienced within an Afro-American frame of reference, such as the "haints"[1] or having "roots"[2] worked on them, which are not part of cultural background of the conventional mental health professional.

While the mental illness model has come under severe criticism from Black psychologists and is regarded in some quarters as a "myth" (Szasz, 1961), it should be pointed out that during its inception in the early part of the twentieth century the mental illness model was regarded as a major revolution, a humanitarian step forward from the earlier divine curse, demonology, and devil possession theories. Ironically, however, there is one stong common bond between the demonology and mental illness theories: both points of view see the locus of psychological disorder as being inside the person.

In the Black community, there is no need to adopt a model of psychological services based on the concept of mental deviance. The

---

[1]*Haints* is a term used in Black folklore to indicate that a hex or evil spell has been put on a person.
[2]*Roots* is a curative term; the root doctor uses roots and herbs to make charms and talismans to combat the haints (May, 1981).

psychological actualization of Black folks cannot occur by any conception of mental health that is oversaturated with images of pathology, deviance, and abnormality, nor can the quality of life in the Black community be improved by models that assign the blame for the poverty in deteriorating urban environments on the victims (Ryan, 1971). With its emphasis on interdependence, closeness, and the essential human likeness, even in the context of manifest differences, the Afro-American world view permits a greater tolerance of diversity and makes it less necessary to set up diagnostic systems, treatment modalities, and elaborate behavior modification systems to regulate and control the behavior of those who are perceived as different. Mental health for Blacks can be defined as having the opportunity to actualize a wide range of intrapersonal, interpersonal, and socioeconomic options throughout the life cycle, free from the artificial barriers created by racial oppression. This definition is consistent with Afro-American values, it is not entrenched in a philosophy of human abnormality or psychopathology, and it identifies racism as the major impediment to psychological wellness in the Black community. To insure that Black people will have a maximum range of psychosocial options, racial oppression as it operates through the major institutions of American life must be sought out and eliminated (Nobles, 1976), a charge equivalent in magnitude to the preventive mental health mandate issued by John Kennedy in 1963.

Accomplishing the task of eliminating institutional racism cannot occur without drastic changes in America's social systems. Social systems and institutions such as education, law enforcement, welfare and health care, transportation, philanthropic foundations, the mass media, and the public and private employment sector, because they have the power to control and restrict access to opportunity, affect the daily lives of Black people. Black psychologists in conjunction with other mental health professionals, civic groups, and elected officals are evolving at the national, regional, and local levels an activist strategy based on a combination of political pressure, legislative action, and objective evidence to compel the policy-making bodies of opportunity-controlling institutions and social systems to be more responsive to the needs of the Black community.

COMMUNITY PSYCHOLOGY

The community psychology model with its emphasis on creating more responsive social systems and institutions most closely approximates the activist style and preventive objectives of Black psychology. The community psychological approach differs from the traditional clinical model in the sense that the community psychologist does not wait for the individual patient to walk in for treatment (Zax and Specter, 1974). The community psychologist reaches out to the community, or service catchment area as it is called, with a coordinated package of preventive mental health services designed to improve the psychological well-being of people across the life cycle. A typical community psychology program operating out of community mental health centers in a Black neighborhood such as Westside in San Francisco and Garfield Park in Chicago is likely to be involved in preschool activities for young children, parent development, couples workshops, tutoring for school-age children, cultural awareness training for teachers, continuing education for mental health professionals, preemployment classes for adolescents and adults, and social activities for senior citizens. At the same time the staff is engaged in monitoring and working as a liaison with educational, social service, law enforcement, and employment agencies. The community is the client and the Black community psychologist is like a social engineer who orchestrates a variety of functions involving several levels of social systems that impinge on the psychological well-being of Black folks. Through its education and consultive services the comprehensive community mental health center is the umbrella agency that normally sponsors these outreach and liaison efforts. The comprehensive community mental health centers, funded by a combination of federal, state, and local sources, are required to offer a complete package of mental health services, which in addition to education and consultation include inpatient and outpatient treatment, partial hospitalization, and emergency services (Murrell, 1978).

For a community mental health center to be maximally effective, it is imperative that the community perspective be reflected in the design and delivery of services. Too often in the past, service models have been developed to do things *for* Black folks rather than with them. Ideally, a community mental health center in the Black community is a cooperative effort with mental health professionals and community people as coequal partners, with community representation at every level of policy making and service delivery. Prior to the advent of the comprehensive mental health care centers in the Black community in the late 1960s, there existed and still exists an informal network of individuals, extended family groups, churches, and social organizations who have been looking out for the mental health needs of the community. These indigenous service providers and individual folk psychologists since the plantation days have been teaching people how to parent, settling family arguments, helping young people get started, calming people during periods of crisis, and providing information through the grapevine about what's going down, how to find a job, and how to deal with "the man's" social service agencies and the criminal justice system. They know what the community needs, have a high level of credibility based on a track record of successful performance, and have a good knowledge of what programs are likely to work built up through years of field testing the programs through direct experience. An interdependent working relationship with these indigenous groups can provide the community mental health center in the Black community with credibility, political support, and expert counsel on program development. The professional staff can in turn provide resources and technical assistance to community groups in areas such as grant-writing skills, funding sources, and office space.

The church elders, grandmothers, curb-stone psychologists, folk healers, spiritualists, tea-leaf readers, psychic Madam Neptunes, and Brother Zoros who have already been operating as care givers should be incorporated into meaningful policy-making and service-provider roles with the Black community mental health system, which is normally done by hiring them as paraprofessionals and community aides. The idea of Black professionals and community mental health paraprofessionals working as coequals may sound good on paper, but it is difficult to achieve in practice. Too often, a continuous source of friction has developed between the two groups regarding expertise, power, and who has the final authority in decision-making situations, with the end result being that the paraprofessionals are regulated to dead-end positions and lack a real voice in policy making. A comprehensive mental health center has the responsibility to avoid dead-end roles for community people by developing a process, conjointly with academic degree-granting institutions, which leads to increasing levels of certification, expertise and financial remuneration through a combination of experience-based credits, in-service training, and job-related competency exams. Increasing the expertise and employability of community people through an experience-based competency and training approach was the original career ladder concept put forth in the Great Society's *New Careers for the Poor* (Pearl and Riessman, 1965). New careers for Black poor folks proved to be more a myth than a reality. Certification boards, professional organizations, and degree-granting institutions were reluctant to create more flexible pathways into the world of advanced degrees required for licensure as a mental health professional.

There is a vast amount of undeveloped talent in the Black community, particularly among the youth, who could increase their range of options by being trained for careers in the expanding spectrum of mental health and health-related fields, not only as practitioners but as administrators, researchers, health planners, teachers, and systems managers. A community mental health system has the opportunity to provide Black youth with direct exposure to prospective careers, role models, and informational networks in mental health and related fields through part-time jobs as peer counselors, case worker aides, research assistants, admission clerks, and general office workers. Black youth need this direct exposure to concrete experiences, combined with Black role models, of how career fields operate because they seldom have the opportunity to acquire first-hand preprofessional training in the course of their daily lives. There is also a critical shortage of fully licensed Black mental health professionals who know the Black community from the experiential perspective of having grown up in it. Early exposure of inner city youth to mental health careers can serve as a long-range recruiting mechanism to decrease the shortage of mental health professionals who have a mixture of formal training and direct experience gained by living in the community.

The dimensions of training for community mental health systems extend beyond inner city youth and community people.

Graduate and preprofessional students, their teachers, and established mental health practitioners, Black and non-Black, can increase their understanding of the issues involved in preventive services, diagnoses, treatment, and in the administration of the overall delivery system by participating in field experiences, internships, practicums, seminars, and continuing education workshops sponsored by Black-oriented community mental health centers. The educational outreach necessary to increase the awareness of current and future professionals about Black-related mental health issues can be expanded by training affiliations between teaching institutions and community health centers that allow for the interchange of staff in teaching roles, clinical supervision, and consultation.

The job of improving the quality of mental health services in the Black community cannot be accomplished in isolation from the spheres of influence in the community at large. The Black mental health center is in a position to provide leadership in creating a more sophisticated consciousness of the issues by facilitating communication between the major spheres of influence, as represented by community people, youth, students in preparation for mental health careers, established minority and nonminority professionals, social activists, university faculty, traditional agencies, funding sources, and the political power brokers.

DIRECT CLINICAL SERVICES AND PSYCHOTHERAPY WITH THE BLACK CLIENT

Even in the most responsive outreach, growth-oriented, preventive community mental health system, there is still a need for direct clinical services. People are going to be faced with personal crisis, periods of extreme distress, and in the normal passages of the life cycle will come to junctures where they will want to use the help of a mental health professional to sort out and cope more effectively with events in their psychological space. Direct clinical assistance is normally provided through inpatient, outpatient, partial hospitalization and twenty-four-hour emergency services; the need for psychological services in the Black community does not stop at 5:00 P.M. and on weekends. Since many community residents may feel uneasy sharing their private concerns with mental health center staff members during their initial visit and are not familiar with the system of intake interviews, assessment and mental status examination, intervention planning, and treatment, the process should be demystified by giving them clear, understandable, honest feedback during each transaction, using a community person as an interpreter if necessary (Sue and Sue, 1977).

Psychotherapy involving a direct face-to-face relationship with the therapist is a standard fare of clinical services. In order to increase their effectiveness in working with Black clients, therapists, Black and non-Black, need to be cognizant of four major issues: the impact of oppression on the lives of Black people, Afro-American psychological perspectives as a source of strength, Afro-American language styles, and the identity concerns that come about as the result of the admixture of Afro-American and Euro-American influences. These issues cut across all therapeutic formats and orientations—group, individual, short-term, long-term, cognitive, behavioral, transactional, psychodynamic, reality, existential, and client-centered.

To genuinely understand the Black client in the context of American society, the therapist should try to fathom the psychological meaning of the rage, sorrow, disappointment, and distrust Black people have felt as a consequence of three and a half centuries of victimization. Most Black adults live in a three-generational space. They can remember what happened to their parents and what is happening to themselves; they can see that the productivity of their children is being hampered by the same insidious racist forces. These feelings of rage, distrust, and sorrow are legitimate (Grier and Cobbs, 1968), they are likely to be expressed within the therapeutic situation, and they cannot be explained away as evidence of severe maladjustment or neurotic manifestations of transference.

Therapists must not get so caught up in understanding and identifying with the Black client as the victim that they fail to see Blacks as worthwhile human beings who have the capacity to grow and develop the strengths necessary to take charge of their lives. Sometimes both white liberals and Black radicals, without fully realizing it, forget that Black people have strengths, and they are unable to establish a balance between seeing Blacks as victims and as resourceful human beings. They get caught up in the assumption that a lifetime of living in an oppressive society has produced an irreversible mark of oppression, a crippled, permanently damaged personality (Block, 1980; Griffith and Jones, 1979). A second error that white therapists sometimes make in the white–Black treatment situation is what Vontress (1971) has termed the great white father syndrome. In the great white father syndrome therapists take the omnipotentlike position that they know what is best for the client, that their judgment is superior, and that the client should passively follow their advice with respectful appreciation for their benevolence.

The Afro-American cultural heritage represents a primary potential source of strengths for Black clients. The emphasis on emotional vitality, resilience, overcoming tragedy, and renewal in Afro-American life styles can provide the psychological foundation for healthy living. The therapist who has developed an awareness of the psychological dimensions of Afro-American culture is in a position to help the patient identify this vitality, capacity for resilience, and ability to cope in their own psychological space. Close interpersonal relationships, mutual aid, collective survival, and interdependence are a vital part of the Afro-American experience base (Nobles, 1976). Being connected to others through extended family groups, social networks, and oral information banks enhances the patient's ability to cope with the effects of oppression and serves as a protective barrier against loneliness, isolation, and alienation. The maintenance of support systems and interdependent relationships with others is a sign of ego strength in Black patients (Block, 1980) that ought to be acknowledged and encouraged rather than interpreted as evidence of dependency needs. Therapists who work with Black clients should be aware of community support groups that can provide their clients with assistance in employment, financial benefits, legal aid, child care, and other social services.

Familiarity with Black expressive patterns is indispensable for therapists working in the Black community. Meaningful communication between patient and therapist cannot take place if the therapist misunderstands the imagery, analogies, and nuances that are being conveyed by Black language styles. A classic case of how misunderstanding of Black communications styles can generate pathological labeling on the part of a naive white therapist is presented in a caricature by Allen Wesson (1975). His mythical character is a nineteen-year-old ghetto youth who is making his mandatory visit to a psychiatrist's office as directed by his probation officer. He immediately starts talking about "stone foxes," not being able to get his "shit together," doing the "break down" and the "penguin," "hearing sounds over the wire," being a "bad mother," and "fucking with pigs."[3] The fictional white psychiatrist begins to think in terms of the patient interacting with animals, having diarrhea, a mental breakdown, dancing with animals, hearing hallucinations over a wire, confusing himself as a mother, and making love to pigs.

While Wesson's caricature is overdrawn to make the point, he is correct in his accusation that non-Black therapists and some middle-class Black therapists have trouble figuring out what Black people are talking about, and the nature of the social dynamics involved in playing the Dozens, bad mouthin', sweet mouthin', lugg droppin', cappin', rhapsodizin', signifyin', mumblin', jonnin', and coppin' an attitude. This is not to suggest that therapists try to come on as culturally hip by imitating speakers of Black English. There is a difference between linguistic receptiveness and shallow expressive imitations. Black clients are apt to regard linguistic hipness on the part of the therapist as first-class phoniness and will be reluctant to put their trust in someone who shows such blatant insincerity. Since most systems of therapy involve working with highly personal communications, it would seem difficult for the therapy to move forward in cases where the patient doesn't trust the therapist or feel confident in the therapist's ability to understand the meaning of what's being expressed.

Black people are exposed to an admixture of Afro-American and Euro-American values in the course of formulating their identity, aspirations, and values. As a result of this dual exposure, they will face critical periods where they need to sort out, clarify, and readjust the balance between these two different world views. Identity-related concerns tend to surface during the late adolescent–early

[3]Alan Wesson, "The Black Man's Burden: the White Clinician", *The Black Scholar*, 1975, *(6)*, pp. 13–18. Reprinted by permission.

adult period for most Blacks and somewhat later for upwardly mobile Black adults. The latter, after having achieved a measure of economic and material success, are beginning to have second thoughts about who they are, what is important to them, and where they are going.

Late adolescents and young adults who are struggling with identity-related issues are usually trying to combine what they perceive as the best of the two worlds. They want to make it in the economic mainstream, yet at the same time they want to retain the openness, genuineness, concern for others, and vitality they have internalized growing up in the Black community. Upwardly mobile, success-oriented Black adults, on the other hand, may deny that their reasons for coming to therapy have anything to do with a conflict in cultural values. In the initial phase of therapy, these brothers and sisters tend to present themselves in a manner analogous to the preencounter stage in Cross's (1980) levels of Black awareness. They have a belief in the superiority of Euro-American values, go to great lengths to convince the therapist that they are human beings who just happen to be Black, claim they can't understand what Blackness is all about, and feel that social problems in America involving Black folks could be resolved if the victims would work harder, develop a future orientation, have fewer babies, and learn to speak right. Therapists unwittingly contribute to this illusion of color blindness (Thomas and Sillen, 1972) by refusing to acknowledge the realities of Black life in America. Attitudes on the part of the therapist that color doesn't make a difference or that Black patients are just like any other patients not only deny the authenticity of Blackness (Sager et al., 1970) but work against the patients' moving toward rediscovering and reintegrating Black values into their life space. It is not up to the therapist to decide the best balance between Afro-American and Euro-American value systems for any given patient. The therapist should be guided by the thesis that Afro-American values can make a significant contribution to psychologically healthy living and that denying a major area of one's existence is not consistent with the principles for sound mental health.

Throughout the discussion of psychotherapy with the Black client, I have alluded to the impact of racial and cultural differences between therapists and clients in the therapeutic process. A growing body of evidence suggests that racial and cultural differences have a definite impact on the process and outcome of psychotherapy. In her review of racial and sociocultural effects in psychotherapy, Block (1980) concluded that when the therapeutic dyad contains a Black patient and a white therapist, Black patients tend to have lower expectations, experience less trust and empathy, feel less understood, and are reluctant to engage in self-disclosure. The findings of Griffith and Jones (1979) concerning the effect of racial and sociocultural differences on premature termination, rapport, depth of exploration, and client satisfaction in psychotherapy support Block's observations. Other studies indicate that as compared to white patients, Black patients are more likely to be seen initially during periods of crisis, more likely to drop out of therapy after the first interview, spend a significantly shorter time in therapy, and discontinue treatment before a mutual termination date is reached (Sue, 1977; Sue et al., 1974).

It seems apparent from the research on race effects in the Black-white therapy dyad that there is a significant psychological and sociocultural distance between Black patients and white therapists that needs to be resolved before therapists will be able to improve their effectiveness in working with Black clients. Therapists can take active steps to decrease the sociocultural distance between themselves and Black patients by developing a consciousness of Afro-American history, expressive patterns, life styles, psychological perspectives, cultural values, and identity issues.

THE ACTUALIZING BLACK

Implicit in any cultural frame of reference, mental health delivery system, and psychotherapeutic model is a definition and set of assumptions about what constitutes a psychologically healthy, actualizing adult. The picture of the psychologically healthy, actualizing Black adult inferred from the Afro-American ethos is that of a person who has internalized an attitude towards self, others, and life in general characterized by vitality, interdependence, mastery of the oral tradition, resourcefulness, and an appreciation of the Afro-American heritage. These characteristics cut across socioeconomic lines, presume some exposure to Afro-American psychological perspectives, but do not imply a total rejection of Euro-American values.

The psychologically healthy Black who has interpreted the Afro-American ethos into his or her life space is able to maintain a zest and enthusiasm for living that is brought about by being open to the renewal experiences of joy, comedy, sensuality, caring, and strength in the face of adversity. He or she accepts as a given that unavoidable pain, struggle, disappointment, and tragedy are necessary for personal growth. This is simply the way things are, nobody gets away clean. He or she is able to experience compassion and sadness without being paralyzed by guilt, shame, despair, and rage. He or she can cry without losing sight of laughter.

The psychologically healthy black is open to self, in touch with others, and willing to reach out and establish close relationships. Physical closeness, tenderness, touching, and sensualilty are valued. The person understands the principle of give and take in close, interdependent relationships, and there is a low quotient of narcissism. He or she draws strength from the realization of not being alone, of being part of a larger, shared cultural heritage, and can identify with the liberation struggle of Black Americans. Because of this shared reality, he or she can establish an easy communication and rapport with other Afro-Americans and blend into extended family groups, quasi-family groups, and social networks.

The psychologically healthy Black is attuned to the language patterns of Black folks, knows how to tap into the historical and contemporary information being transmitted in the Black community by the oral tradition, doesn't need anyone to interpret what's going down when Black expressive styles are being used, and is conscious of the power of the spoken word to heal, inspire, teach, control, and get you over.

Psychologically healthy blacks are resourceful, inventive, imaginative, and enterprising in their approach to life. They are not immobilized or devastated by the realities of oppression in American life. They have learned through the course of a lifetime that if they are going to have an equal range of options they have to depend on their own resources to create them, the master is not going to do it for them. Historically, Blacks have shown a remarkable degree of resourcefulness and imagination by creating an entire cultural base under the nose of the oppressor without the oppressor being aware of what was happening (Fredrickson, 1976).

From the beginning of slavery forward, Black people through successive cycles of oppression, resistance, transcendence, and retrogression have been able to keep on pushin'. There seems to be a persistent "movin' on up" theme in the Black experience base, an ascendant motivation that is reflected in the inventiveness, determination, and resourcefulness of Black problem-solving behavior at all levels—from welfare grandmothers feeding their families on limited budgets, to brothers figuring out a way to connect with sisters who act like they don't want to be bothered, to Black professionals getting together with community people in order to plan strategies to deal with "the man." The resourceful Black person's attitude is like Daddy King's (1980), "I can handle it."

As actualizing Blacks move through the adult life cycle, they develop a guiding philosophy that reflects an appreciation for the wisdom contained in Afro-American folklore that can only come through direct experience. By learning to absorb, overcome, keep on keepin' on, and keep the faith through sorrow, tragedy, and disappointment, actualizing Blacks develop an unshakable inner resolve. They are proud of being Black, not afraid of being destroyed by racism, do not need the personal validation of Euro-Americans, and no longer entertain illusions about fair play as the cornerstone of American life. They have established a workable balance between the Afro-American and Euro-American value systems in their internal space. They feel a need to be in touch with the tribal elders and a responsibility to pass on what they have experienced to the next generation. They have a three-generation time perspective, are not apprehensive about the prospect of aging, and have mastered the fear of death by learning to celebrate life fully in the present.

REFERENCES

ADEBIMPE, VICTOR. "Overview: White Norms in Psychiatric Diagnosis of Black Patients," *American Journal of Psychiatry*, 138, no. 3, (March 1981), 279–285.

BLOCK, CAROLYN. "Black Americans and the Cross Cultural Counseling and Psychotherapy Experience" in A. J. Marsella, and P. Pederson, eds., *Cross Cultural Counseling and Psychotherapy: Foundations, Evolutions and Cultural Considerations.* Elmsford, N.Y.: Pergamon Press, 1981.

CROSS, WILLIAM. "Models of Nigrescence: A Literature Review," in R. L. Jones ed., *Towards a Black Psychology* (2nd ed.). New York: Harper & Row, 1980.

FREDRICKSON, GEORGE. "The Gutman Report," *New York Review,* September 30, 1976, pp. 18–22, 27.

FROMM, ERIC. *The Sane Society.* New York: Holt, Rinehart & Winston, 1955.

GRIER, WILLIAM, and COBBS, PRICE. *Black Rage.* New York: Basic Books, 1968.

GRIFFITH, M. S. "The influence of Race on Psychotherapeutic Relationship," *Psychiatry,* 40, no. 1 (1977), 27–40.

GRIFFITH, M. S., and JONES, E.E. "Race and Psychotherapy: Changing Perspectives," in J. H. Mosserman, ed., *Current Psychiatric Therapies,* Vol. 18. New York: Grune & Stratton, 1979.

KENNEDY, JOHN. "Message from the President of the United States Relative to Mental Illness and Mental Retardation." 88th Congress, 1st Session, House of Representatives, *Document No. 58.* Washington, D.C.: U.S. Government Printing Office, 1963.

KING, L. "Social and Cultural Issues in Psychopathology," *Annual Review of Psychology,* 29, (1978), 405–433.

KING, MARTIN LUTHER, SR. *Daddy King.* New York: Morrow, 1980.

MAY, LEE. "Hex Appeal: Vodoo Casts Its Spell on Many in U.S.," *Los Angeles Times,* August 13, 1981, Part I, pp. 1, 16.

MEMMI, ALFRED. *The Colonizers and Colonized.* Boston: Beacon Press, 1965.

MURRELL, STANLEY. *Community Psychology and Social Systems: A Conceptual Framework and Intervention Guide.* New York: Behavioral Publications, 1978.

NOBLES, WADE. "Black People in White Insanity : An Issue for Community Mental Health," *Journal of Afro-American Issues,* 4, no. 1 (Winter 1976), 21–27.

PEARL, ARTHUR, and RIESSMAN, FRANK. *New Careers for the Poor.* New York: Free Press, 1965.

RYAN, W. *Blaming the Victim*. New York: Pantheon, 1971.

SAGER, C.; BRAYBOY, T. L.; AND WAXENBERG, B. M. *The Black Ghetto Family in Therapy*. New York: Grove Press, 1970.

SUE, DERALD, and SUE, DAVID. "Barriers to Effective Cross-Cultural Counseling," *Journal of Counseling Psychology*, 24, no. 5 (1977), 420–429.

SUE, STANLEY. "Community Mental Health Services to Minority Groups," *American Psychologist*, 32 (1977), 616–624.

SUE, S.; McKINNEY, H.; ALLEN, P.; and HALL, J. "Delivery of Community Mental Health Services to Black Clients," *Journal of Consulting and Clinical Psychology*, 42 (1974), 794–801.

SZASZ, THOMAS. *The Myth of Mental Illness: Foundations of a Theory of Personal Conduct*. New York: Harper & Hoeber, 1961.

THOMAS, A., and SILLEN, S. *Racism and Psychiatry*. New York: Brunner/Mazel, 1972.

VONTRESS, C. E. *Counseling Negroes*. New York: Houghton Mifflin, 1971.

WESSON, ALAN. "The Black Man's Burden: The White Clinician," *Black Scholar*, 6 (1975), 13–18.

ZAX, MELVIN, and SPECTER, GERALD. *An Introduction to Community Psychology*. New York: John Wiley, 1974.

CHAPTER SEVEN

CONCLUSIONS AND DIRECTIONS FOR THE FUTURE

THE BLACKANIZING OF AMERICA

What has gone unnoticed by many observers is the movement of the Euro-American ethos, life styles, psychology, and mental health orientations in the direction of more closely approximating Afro-American norms, values, and behaviors. Without sufficiently acknowledging the possibility of a reverse acculturation effect, Euro-Americans are showing a likeness to Black folks. In *The Greening of America*, Reich (1970) describes a progression of American consciousness through three stages during the past two centuries. Consciousness I represents the mid-nineteenth-century view of America as a budding industrial society, the period of the robber barons, characterized by a philosophy of ruthless competition, economic exploitation, individualism, and psychological repression. Consciousness II, covering the first half of the twentieth century, is the era of the corporate state and the New Deal with an emphasis on meritocracy, survival of the organization, and a bureaucratic concern for the less fortunate. Consciousness III, a vision of society that is in a state of becoming, is typified by humanitarian concern for others, genuineness, awareness of the inner space of feelings, and a community of brotherhood. Consciousness III strongly resembles the values of realness, psychological openness, interdependence, mutual aid, and cooperativeness embedded in the Afro-American ethos.

The music, dance, hair styles, and informal language of the majority culture, particularly among young adults, is becoming blacker as Euro-Americans try to figure out what's happening, where they are coming from, how to get down, and how to get up and boogie. The activism of the Black revolution has come home to mainstream America as women, youth, Vietnam veterans, handicapped people, the aging Gray Panthers, and non-Black ethnic minority groups have adopted the protest strategies and networking techniques of the civil rights movement.

There have been corresponding changes in the field of psychology. The existential, self-actualization, and human potentials movements have spoken out against the view that human condition is dominated by repressive internal and external forces. Human existence is depicted in terms of freedom, vitality, psychological openness, realness, the need for close relationships with others, the inevitability of tragedy and death, and the potential for growth and renewal of the human spirit through loss, intimacy, joy, and laughter.

In the field of mental health there has been a gradual movement away from the obsession with abnormality and classification of pathology, coupled with a greater respect for the underlying commonalities within the diversity of human experience. Holistic concepts of mental health stress the unity of mind and body, prevention, wellness, and the human capacity to develop psychological strengths and effective coping mechanisms. Community psychologists have advocated the need for more responsive support systems and social institutions.

Changes in the Euro-American ethos, values, life styles, and psychological concepts have not occurred in a straight, linear fashion. There have been stops, starts, retrograde motions, and attempts to return to the old days of human oppression, exploitation, individualism, and psychological repression. Nonetheless, something in the way of a significant shift in psychosocial forces that may be more latent than visible is working its way into the fabric of America. Sociologist Daniel Yankelovich (1981), basing his findings on national surveys and numerous oral histories, feels that Americans are expressing a longing for connectedness and are fearful of ending up alone and empty-handed. In the second stage of its development, the "me first" generation is reaching out to establish closer bonds with those around them.

THE EVOLUTION OF ETHNICITY IN PSYCHOLOGY

Black psychology has been the forerunner of an ethnic and cultural awareness in psychology that is working its way into the literature on child development, self-image, family dynamics, education, communication patterns, counseling and psychotherapy, and mental health delivery systems. The blossoming of Black psychology has been followed by the assertion on the part of Asian American (Sue and Wagner, 1973), Chicano (Martinez, 1977) and Native American (Richardson, 1981) psychologists that sociocultural differences in the experiential field must be considered as legitimate correlates of behavior. The development of an ethnic dimension in psychology suggests that other nonwhite Americans want to take the lead in defining themselves rather than continue the process of being defined by the deficit-deficiency models of the majority culture. The evolution of the ethnic cultural perspective enlarges the scope of psychology. It is a corrective step that will reduce psychology's reliance on obsolete and inaccurate stereotypes in defining minority people.

WHERE DO WE GO FROM HERE?

In the preceding chapters I have tried to identify the basic psychological dimensions and recurring themes in the Afro-American frame of reference and to describe how the Afro-American psychological perspective is expressed in language, family dynamics, child rearing, male-female relationships, education, and mental health. Further research is needed to establish a more precise definition of each of these dimensions, how they are interrelated, and under what psychosocial and environmental conditions behaviors associated with Afro-American psychological perspectives are likely to be observed. The long-term research efforts of Nobles (1978) and McAdoo (1979) on the Black family, Cross (1978) on levels of Black awareness, Banks (1976) on self-image, and Williams (1974) on intelligence show considerable promise for providing answers to complex theoretical questions and can serve as a prototype for future research in other areas.

More needs to be known about the relationship between Afro-American psychological perspectives and socioeconomic class, what changes have occurred in Black values during the rural to urban transition, how the Afro-American frame of reference is transmitted to children, and how children filter out negative ideas regarding Blackness communicated by Euro-American society. Although this book has concentrated on the differences between Blacks and whites, it is obvious that the two groups share some areas of a common social-psychological space. What are the primary common psychological characteristics between Blacks and whites, and for Blacks, what is a healthy integration of the commonalities and differences?

The picture of blackness being projected in the literature of psychology seems to be changing from the deficit-deficiency, victim analysis, "Mark of Oppression" (Kardiner and Ovesey, 1951) syndrome to a discovery of strengths in Black personality traits, behaviors, and attitudes. Block (1980) and Cross (1978), in their respective reviews of studies on psychotherapy and identity, see the shift to a more positive conception of Blackness as a consequence of the Black revolution, with the 1960s representing a convenient time frame to mark off the before and after periods. The presence of the Association of Black Psychologists in an advocacy role has no doubt contributed to the changing conception of Blackness in psychology.

Future studies are needed to determine other sources, correlates, and causative agents responsible for the new psychological images of blackness. Have Black folks changed as a result of an increase in positive identity brought about by the Black revolution, or are contemporary researchers creating fewer errors of transubstantiation by using a more culturally appropriate frame of reference to examine Black behavior? How is the view of Afro-American psychology being received by non-Black behavioral scientists? Is it being incorporated into graduate training programs, seminars, and continuing education programs, and are attitudes, beliefs and strategies for working with Blacks in actual practice also changing?

Black psychologists have developed a multitude of strategies, techniques, and paradigms to deal with issues in child rearing, self-concept formation, family interaction, male–female relationships, intellectual and diagnostic assessment, education, psychotherapy, community mental health, forensic psychology, and the broader question of creating decisive changes in social systems. Those techniques and strategies that show the greatest potential for increasing the range of options for Black folks, improving the quality of life, and making social systems more responsive should be identified and incorporated into a comprehensive, long-term, applied research program designed to reach the maximum number of Black communities.

REFERENCES

BANKS, W. CURTIS. "White Preference in Blacks: A Paradigm in Search of a Phenomenon," *Psychological Bulletin*, 83, no. 6 (1976), 1179–1186.

BLOCK, CAROLYN. "Black Americans and the Cross Cultural Counseling Experience" in A. J. Marsella, and P. Pedersen, eds., *Cross Cultural Counseling and Psychotherapy: Foundations, Evaluations and Cross Cultural Considerations*. Elmsford, N.Y.: Pergamon Press, 1980.

CROSS, WILLIAM. "Black Family and Identity: A Literature Review," *Western Journal of Black Studies*, 2, no. 2 (Summer 1978), 111–124.

KARDINER, ABRAHAM, and OVESEY, LIONEL. *The Mark of Oppression*. New York: W. W. Norton & Co. 1951.

MARTINEZ, J. L., JR., ed. *Chicano Psychology*. New York: Academic Press, 1977.

McADOO, HARRIET. "Black Kinship," *Psychology Today*, May 1979, pp. 67–69, 79, 110.

NOBLES, WADE. "Toward an Empirical and Theoretical Framework for Defining Black Families," *Journal of Marriage and Family*, November 1978, pp. 679–688.

REICH, CHARLES. T*he Greening of America*. New York: Random House, 1970.

RICHARDSON, EDWIN. "Cultural and Historical Perspectives in Counseling American Indians" in D. W. Sue, *Counseling the Culturally Different: Theory and Practice*. New York: John Wiley, 1981.

SUE, STANLEY, and WAGNER, NATHANIEL, eds. *Asian Americans: Psychological Perspectives*. Palo Alto, Calif.: Science and Behavior Books, 1973.

WILLIAMS, ROBERT. "The Problem of Match and Mismatch" pp. 67–75 in L. Miller, ed., *The Testing of Black Children*. Englewood Cliffs, N.J.: Prentice-Hall, 1974.

YANKELOVICH, DANIEL. *New Rules: Searching for Self-Fulfillment in a World Turned Upside Down*. New York: Random House, 1981.

GLOSSARY OF BLACK SOCIAL-LINGUISTIC TERMS

*Adopted from E. Smith "Evolution and Continuing Presence of the Oral Tradition in Black America" (Unpublished Doctoral Dissertation, University of California—Irvine, 1974). Reprinted by permission.

GLOSSARY OF BLACK
SOCIAL-LINGUISTIC TERMS

BAD MOUTH, BAD MOUTHIN'

1. An Africanism meaning to speak against or make unfavorable remarks about someone or something; to put a curse on someone; negative idle gossiping, slander, defamation of one's character, to calumniate one's escutcheon.

    Syn: lug droppin', larcen-up, talkin' stuff, buck one's luck ('buck yo' luck').

    Situation: A person has accomplished a commendable deed or performed an extraordinary task. A pseudofriend, who is actually envious, smiles and praises him to his face but berates and belittles him behind his back by 'puttin' the bad mouth on him.'

2. Malicious gossip. (Majors, 1971)

3. To talk about someone maliciously. (Haskins and Butts, 1973)

4. "Slander, abuse, gossip" (both noun and verb). Cf. similar use of *Mandingo da-jugu* and Hausa *naugum-baki*, "slander, abuse," (lit. *bad mouth* in both cases). Note also *fat mouth*. (Dalby, 1972, p. 177)

5. The telling of stories that may be true but that reflect adversely on a person's character or reputation; e.g., 'He's putting the *bad mouth* on her now'; to gossip about someone.

    Syn: Tear apart. (Roberts, 1971).

BASE, BASIN'

1. To confront or have a catharsis on someone; to come down front with an issue in an untactful manner; to get right to the basics.

Situation: Two people have had a long and sustained friendship, courtship, or acquaintance, e.g., roomates or coworkers. They have done a lot of favors for each other and have each ignored a lot of the other's foibles. A situation arises where an argument ensues. They begin to throw up the past and blurt out deep-seated and basic dislikes they have harbored for each other.

Syn: To jam, splib, blow on, fat mouth, front off, cap.

2. To verbally disparage someone, to base on someone. (Folb, 1972)

3. To come down hard on someone; to get to the base of the problem in a ruthless way. (Andrews and Owens, 1973).

BLOW, BLOW ON

1. to confront a person face to face with a relentless interrogation; a sensitivity session or encounter group.

Syn: To base, fat mouth, sound on, group, jam, scream, sound.

Situation: A person is confronting someone about a rumor that's being spread. They engage in a shouting match and are standing in such close proximity to each other that each can feel the other's breath (or often saliva).

2. To be particularly aggressive verbally with another, esp., a female; e.g., to blow on someone; to monopolize a conversation with the intensity and verbosity of your comments; to put down another person verbally. (Folb, 1972).

CALL AND RESPONSE (said to be an Africanism)

1. To bear witness or cosign verbally.

2. The call and response is also the style of most Black orators and their audiences.

Situation: The call and response is both secular and nonsecular. In the religious context, the call and response occurs in hymns as well as during the Black preacher's sermon. In the secular context, the call and response occurs in Black civic and political meetings and rallies. Call and response in songs is typified in the refrain that follows the lead singer.

CAPPIN'

There are two distinct meanings for the word *cappin'*: one represents the verbal art of the Black con artist or hustler; the other represents a style of Black adolescent behavior.

1. To distract the companion of an intended victim by the use of nonsensical rhetoric; the nonsensical conversation or rhetoric serves as a 'cap'

to cover up the actual intentions or purposes for which the 'cap man' or his accomplice has made the encounter.

2. A cutting remark made as a comeback to a provocation or put-down. Syn: the Dozens, jonin', signifyin', soundin', basin', woof-in, fat mouthin'.

3. To verbally put down another or another's family (Folb, 1972).

4. cutting someone down with words, usually in a verbally competitive situation. (Andrews and Owens, 1973).

5. CAPPED: excelled, topped (Kochman, 1972, p. 244).

COP A PLEA

1. A penitent plea for leniency; to entreaty or beg for pity or forgiveness; to cop out; to plead to one of many violations for reduced sentence. Syn: soprana, gripping.

Situation: A person is about to leave or has been 'cut loose' by his lover. The rejected lover skillfully and artfully submits arguments (cops a plea) E.g., 'If you leave, I'll die;' 'I'll do anything you say' or 'I'll kill myself,' . etc., to convince his lover that they should stay or get back together.

2. To ask someone to disregard what you just said; almost like a beg to forget. E.g., Don't try to cop a plea on me! (Andrews and Owens, 1973).

3. Now generally used to mean to beg, plead for mercy, and as in, 'Please cop, don't hit me.' (Kochman, 1970).

4. To be verbally evasive (1935–55). (Major, 1970).

COP ON

To talk someone down (Roberts, 1971).

COVER SNATCH, SNATCHIN'

1. To unmask or uncover someone in public; to 'rank' or blow someone's game by revealing some misdeeds or undoings of theirs; to remove a veneer (unlike *frontin off*, which is loud-talkin' a person in a crowd or bad mouthin' behind someone's back, *cover snatchin'* is an expose done more by Black preachers, Black orators, and stand-up-straight Black comics; an ad populum attack by a public speaker or comedian.

Syn: frontin' off, lugg droppin', signifyin', bad mouthin', soundin'.

Situation: A Black Student Union (BSU) member in a prominent position has been Black by day, white by night. The chairman exposes him or her at the BSU meeting.

DOZENS, DIRTY DOZENS

1. Using stylized rhymes, the Dozens is played as a verbal combat or game of one-upsmanship in which two persons (usually adolescents) exchange uncomplementary remarks about each other's parents, re-

latives, or socioeconomic status. The majority of the derogatory remarks are usually about each other's mother.

EXAMPLE: I fucked yo' mama on the piano stool; up jumped a baby playin' the St. Louis Blues.

Syn: Signifiyin', woofin'.

2. The science of disparaging one's ancestors. (Andrews and Owens, 1973)

Syn: Playing the Dozens, playing, sounding, and woofin'. The terms indicate the procedure involved—*playin'* illustrates that a game or contest is being waged; *soundin'* shows that the game is vocal and *wolfin'* or *woofin'* points out the similarity of the procedure to a dog's bark (Abrahams, 1973, p. 47).

4. A word game in which close members of the family are degraded (Haskins and Butts, 1973, p. 84).

5. A very elaborate game traditionally played by Black boys, in which the particpants insult each other's relatives, especially their mothers. The object of the game is to test emotional strength. The first person to give in to anger is the loser. (Major, 1970, p. 46)

DROP A DIME

To inform on someone, usually a bookie, narcotics pushers, or fence, by making an anonymous phone call (which costs a dime) to the police.

Syn: Snitch, give someone up.

Situation: A horse player phones in a bet to her bookie. She wants to play the number six horse in the fifth race. The bookie mistakenly writes the number five horse in the sixth race. It just so happens that the number six horse in the fifth race wins. The bookie refuses to pay. The horse player "drops a dime" on him.

FAT LIP

Obnoxious talk. (Major, 1970, p. 53)

FAT MOUTH, MOUTHIN'

A truculent, scathing and fiercely heated verbal exchange, that inevitably results in a physical encounter. Unlike the dozens, signifyin', or woofin', which are characterized by rhymes and styled phrases that are jokingly exchanged in jest or competition, fat mouthin' denotes a more invective and vituperative verbal exchange.

Situation: Two guys are shooting dice. One loses all his money and accuses the other of having cheated, claiming the dice are crooked. He threatens to kick the other's ass and take his money back. They then engage in a fierce verbal exchange with each other and eventually end up fighting.

FRONT OFF, FRONTIN' OFF

To rebuke or loud talk someone with the intent of embarrassing or making an example of him or her before a crowd; puttin' someone down in order to look big, authoritarian, or to save face.

Situation: A student is late to school. She's scolded by a teacher in front of her classmates and ordered out of the room. The student refuses to leave. The teacher goes and tells the principal. The principal uses the school intercom to call the student to the office and announces over the intercom that the student is going to be suspended. The student was 'fronted off' by the principal.

GATE MOUTH, MOUTHIN'

1 Said of a person who has a reputation of being a gossiper, muck racker, or a rumormonger. Hence, a big mouth literally is a mouth that swings open like a gate.

Syn: Jaw jackin,' stuff towin".

Situation: A person is told something in strictest confidence ("Jes' between me and you and the gate post") and told not to tell a soul. Less than two minutes after she is told the information, she has told three other people.

2 gossiper. (Major, 1971, p. 57)

GIBB' GIBBIN'; JIBBIN'

Probably from jivin'; talkin excessively and extraneously; running off at the mouth nonstop trying to sound intellectual.

Syn: Jaw jackin'.

Situation: Two students are having an intellectual debate in a school cafeteria. When one of the students notices that a girl he wants to impress is listening, he escalates his conversation to keep the girl's attention.

GIBE (same as JIBBIN')

To meddle, tease, or taunt a person to the point of exasperation.

GRIPP, GRIPPIN'

1. A sniveling and whimpering plea for sympathy. A dramatized, hand-wringing entreaty. Unlike copping a plea, which is artistic rappin,' grippin' is a more sycophant pleading.
   Syn: Cop a plea.
   Situation: A child is about to get a whipping for a violation. The child starts pleading for an opportunity to explain. "Please mama, lemme explain. . ." all while being whipped, the child pleads, "Please mama, lemme explain, Ooo, please lemme explain. . ."
2. To beg one's way out of a situation by self-depreciation; e.g., 'Dig him trying to grip that broad.'

Syn: Ralph Bunche. (Roberts, 1971)

3. . . .refers to behavior that stems from fear and a respect for superior power. (Kochman, 1972, p. 255)

GROUP, GROUPED

1 An encounter or sensitivity session.

2. To verbally confront someone with the intent of giving shock therapy.

3. Usually several people verbally interrogating someone who's 'shit ain't together'!

Situation: A brother droppin' reds, stealing from his friends, won't take a bath, etc. Some of his friends get together and verbally come down on him.

Syn: to jam, base.

HIGH SIDIN' (SIGNIN)

1. To tease, berate or poke fun at someone who is in a bad fix or less fortunate; to act haughty, pious, pompous, and innocent; joking and cutting up (from the sidelines) at the expense of another.

Syn: signifyin', hoorahin', woofin', frontin' off.

Situation: A child has recently been rebuked by a parent or teacher for not having done her house or home work. The children who have done their work poke fun, mock the child who is in trouble.

2. Cutting up, having fun at the expense of another. (Cleaver, 1968, p. 27)

3. A made-up signal between two or more people for alertness (high sign).

4. to high sign; to show off what one has, e.g., car, clothes, girl friend, etc.; to display the colors, sign, etc. of one's special group affiliation. (Folb, 1972)

5. A show-offy attitude; when people act like they're better than everyone else, even themselves, they are high signin'. (Andrews and Owens, 1973)

HOORAH, HOORAHIN'

To drive, provoke, or goad someone. When a crowd or group of significant others dares or encourages a person to persist or desist (depending on the situation) by jeering, snickering, or yelling praises.

Syn: high side, signifyin'.

Situation: An authority figure such as a probation counselor in Juvenile Hall orders a youth to cease and desist a disruptive behavior in a very untactful and abrasive manner. The child feels fronted off. The other youths present dare, goad, and encourage him or her to persist, by hoorahin', "Man, I wouldn't take that if I was you."

JAW JACKIN'

1. Verbose, wordy; literally, a sustained up-and-down (jackin') movement of the mandible (jaw); extraneous verbosity, that is, wordiness
   on a matter that is totally irrelevant to the point at hand.

   Syn: talkin' loud'n sayin' nothin', running off at the jibs, gibbin',
   protection talk, grippin'.

   Situation: A student gets called on to make an oral presentation in
   class. She doesn't know the subject matter but talks and talks about what she
   thinks it is.

2. "Flappin' chops"; running off at the mouth; talkin' loud but saying
   nothing.

JEFFIN'

1. Puttin' ole massa on; to clown; the simultaneous shuffling, head
   scratching and rolling one's eyes, and grinning; acting servile or
   obsequious in the presence of whitey; to con ole massa by clowning.

   Situation: A child in custodial detention at Juvenile Hall is told he or
   she can earn brownie points for tidiness, being dutiful and good mannered,
   etc. The child who is overtly dutiful and good mannered and comical in a
   "Roscoe," "Beulah," "Aunt Jemima," demeanor often gets over with the
   probation officers.

   Syn: Playin' a game, showboatin', stuff playin', tommin', brown
   nose.

2. low-level con—tommin'; shuffling with soft-shoe tip.

3. The terms used by the Black to describe the role played before White
   folks in the South. (Kochman, 1972, p. 246)

JIVE, JIVIN'

1 To engage in a phoney put-on; meddle or play practical jokes on or
   with someone; behaving prankishly, not doing one's best at some task;
   continuously putting something off, fooling around.

   Situation: A child brings a dead rat or snake to school and throws it
   on people or puts it in the teacher's desk drawer.

   Syn: Half steppin, hoorahin, shuckin' and jivin', siggin'.

2. A whole lot of talk; an unreliable person; one's personality or belong-
   ings (jive), e.g., 'You better get your jive together.' A persuasive talker
   quick to make commandments but prone to lie and make excuses for
   not delivering; a person who is always late but has a semiplausible
   excuse; a man with many girl friends; one who is not in the know; to
   fool or deceive; to give a girl a line; to be out of step with things.
   (Roberts, 1971)

3. A whole lot of talk. Originally and still used in the sense of *fuck* and
   jazz, i.e., the sexual act.

Syn: Shuckin' and jivin.'

4. to sneer (1920s–1930s); deceit to put someone on (may be a distortion of the English word *jibe*) (1940s–1950s). Often intensified by the suffix *ass,* as in *jive-ass.*

JONIN'

1. An East coast term for playing the dozens; to taunt, ridicule, mock or put someone down verbally.

Situation: Two children are having a verbal dual. One says: 'I fucked yo mama for her birthday—her pussy was so nasty, I had to make her pay.' The other replies: "I fucked yo mama and yo sister Flo—now both the bitches wanna be my whoe."

Syn: The dozens, cappin', signifyin', woofin'.

2. See signifyin'. (Roberts, 1971)

LARCEN, LARCENIN'

1. To maliciously and grudgingly inform on someone.
2. To turn someone in to the police.
3. To spread disparaging information about someone, especially with the intent to injure them in such a way as to cause a loss of (a) money, (b) life, or (c) liberty; to take advantage of a child, the feeble minded, handicapped, or blind.
4. To lie with a malicious intent to take advantage of someone's innocence or ignorance.
5. To betray a trust.

Situation: Two very close friends fall out. One is so bitter he calls the other's husband or wife on the phone and informs about some hanky panky.

Syn: Flyin' under false colors, Lyin', bad mouth, drop a dime, snitch, squeal.

LARCENY

1. To turn against by vocal condemnation.
2. An unkind or evil feeling or open condemnation of another person. (Major, 1970)

LOLLY GAGGIN'

Lolly = tongue; Gag = joke.
Idle conversation or chatter of a group; chit chatting, loitering.

Situation: Boys and girls hang around hot dog stands after school or club members have a conversation under the street lamp on the corner.

Syn: Shuckin' and jivin', rappin'.

LUG DROPPIN'

To tell a joke or make fun of someone by insinuating something in his or her presence without the person's knowing it's directed towards him or her; to subtly drop something embarrassing into a conversation about someone, thus adding insult to an injury; usually prefaced by the remark, "Of course, it ain't none of my business," the comment is dropped into the conversation.

   Situation: Someone's car has been repossessed. The person may or may not know it. A friend finds out and drops this information into a conversation out of context.

   Situation: Someone is dating a married person but doesn't know the person is married. A friend finds out and drops it into a conversation out of context.

LUG

To introduce (a topic, story, etc.) without good reason, into a conversation, discourse, etc. (Webster's)

MACK, MACKIN'

1. Pimp, gigolo, playboy. A marcaroni; an English dandy who affected foreign mannerisms and fashions.
2. A sharp, stylish dresser, said of Black males who usually are hustlers and pimps.
3. To talk well, particularly to a female with the intention of impressing her.
4. Con-game; to swindle, after gaining a person's confidence.

   Situation: A guy driving an Eldorado comes into a cafe. He begins a conversation with a lady. He constantly gazes to the left and right as if something uneventful is about to occur. As he's talkin' he gestures with his hands to show his rings and constantly strokes dust from his cuffs.

   Syn: Pimp talk, sweetmouthin,' rappin', stuff player.
5. Used by the speaker at the beginning of a relationship to create a favorable impression and be persuasive. (Kochman, 1972, p. 243)
6. Both *rappin'* and *mackin'* describe a person of considerable status in the street hierarchy, who, by his lively and persuasive rappin, (*mackin'* is also used in this context) has acquired a stable of girls to hustle for him and give him money. (Kochman, 1972, p. 61)
7. To talk, particularly to a female with the intention of impressing her; to kiss. (Folb, 1972)

MAU MAUIN'

Originally an African liberation organization in Kenya that terrorized whites into submission. Now, seriously threatening Whitey. Blowin on Whitey or those in authority (usually whites), alluding to resort to terror tactics and violence if demands are not met. Distinguished from *selling woof tickets,* which implies no actual intent of carrying out alluded terror.

Situation: The Black Student Union or SLA sends a list of nonnegotiable demands to an official of the power elite. When the power elite refuses to yield to the demands, the group in question resorts to terror tactics against the establishment or power elite.

MUMBLIN'

1. A stylized manner of blank verse "rhapsodizing" in which words are barely audible and unintelligible. The intonation, inflection, and gesticulation, however, convey the meanings of the missing phrases.
2. Talkin under one's breath, grumbling.
3. "Clark Terry," rapping.

Situation: A brother at a record shop wants to talk to a girl but he has no real basis for much conversation. So he approaches her and says: "Ahh .. . (gestures) ... didn't I ... uh, ... (mumbles) ... meet you in Paris ... (gestures) ... ah, (mumbles) ... say, who you here with? ... (mumbles) ... umm ... (mumbles) ... I'm Sweet Peety ... I'm a lady's pet ... (mumbles) ... niggas' threat.

Syn: Mackin', rappin', sweet mouthin'.

PIMP TALK

1. A heavy conversation; said of hustlers and articulate Black males who presumably are so glib and smooth they have beguiled women into prostitution.

Situation: See *mackin'.*

Syn: Mackin', rappin', sweet mouthin', stuff playin'.

2. Affixing of a nonsense syllable to certain syllables of words. (Origin: Chicago).

Syn: mumblin', mackin'. (Haskins and Butts, 1973, p. 85)

PROTECTION TALK

1. Ego-defense conversation; conversation in which the person's remarks are designed to cover up an embarrassing situation. In order to deal with feelings of embarrassment and shame, the defensive person suggests that the whole situation was self-contrived and that the advantage was actually his or hers.
2. A nobody, or a somebody who has fallen, who pretends to be big or great because he or she has or used to have close association with stars and notables.

Situation: A girl gets pregnant while in high school or college. She claims the whole thing is a part of her master plan.

PULL COAT

1. To caution or signal someone to be careful by tugging their coat from behind (nonverbal).
2. To overtly inform or alert someone by systematically explaining in much detail why he or she should not make a particular move (verbal).

Situation: Two guys are at a used car lot. One, interested in a car, selects the car he wants and begins to close the deal. The guy who is purchasing the car asks the dealer about the interest rate. The dealer says 5 percent. The friend asks the dealer what is the APR (Annual Percentage Rate). This is a cue that the dealer is a liar.

RAP, RAPPIN'

1. Originally rhapsodizing; fascinating or dazzling someone with conversation. Hence, to flatter and express deep, sincere devotion to a guy or girl.
2. To woo or flatter with praise, accolades, and amorous expressions of desire.
3. Now, conversation in general.

Situation: A guy calls a girl on the phone. He wants her to be his steady girl. He tells her how different she is from all the girls he met—how intelligent she is, how fine she looks, what a nice personality she has—and he takes two hours to do it.

Syn: Mack, sweet mouthin', pimp talk.

4. A fluent and lively way of talking characterized by a high degree of personal style; e.g., 'He cops a mean rap'.

Syn: Shoot the bull; a conversation with romatic content; the narration of an event; to talk to a person or group, describing or narrating something colorfully; to inform; to talk to a girl with romance in mind. (Roberts, 1971)

5. Conviction of a crime. (Abrahams, 1970, p. 263)
6. To tell the truth, uncluttered and to the point; to talk. (Haskins and Butts, 1973, p. 242)
7. While used synonymously to mean ordinary conversation, *rappin'* is distinctively a fluent and lively way of talking, that is always characterized by a high degree of personal style. Rappin' to a woman is a colorful way of "asking for some pussy." (Kochman, 1972, p. 242)

RHAPSODIZE

To be or to have been fascinated by someone with a heavy rap or conversation.

Situation: A woman waiting at a bus stop is approached by a suave, debonair young man who very excitedly begins to express accolades and praise for her appearance and her charisma; in less than two minutes he has obtained her phone number and address and arranged a dinner date.

RUNNING IT DOWN

1. To very exactly explain to the last detail how something goes or does not go and then repeat the process as a rerun.

    Situation: An automobile accident, fight, shooting, or other un-eventful incident has occurred. A guy sees that someone he knows is already on the scene and he asks him what happened. The person who was a witness or who was on the scene explains in precise detail.

2. Used by ghetto dwellers when they intend to communicate information in the form of an explanation, narrative, giving advice, and the like; *running it down* has basically an informative function, telling somebody something that he or she doesn't know. (Kochman, 1972, p. 254)

3. Keep talkin'; hurry up and tell me. (Haskins and Butts, 1968, p. 86)

SCAT SINGIN' (SKITIN' AND SCATIN')

1. A stylized form of singing jazz; a lyrical improvisation using bound morphemes or nonsense syllables to follow the music scale, e.g., b, d, f, a, c.

    Situation: When singers are singin a song that they have forgotten or never knew the lyrics to, they often improvise by singing "shoop-do-be-dop-da-ba-dop," etc., humming along with the band in a way that no can tell. E.g., the Pointer Sisters, Ella Fitzgerald, Sara Vaughn, Ross of Lambert, Hendericks and Ross.

2. SCAT: (1920s) generally attributed to Louis Armstrong, who, when he forgot the words of a song would make up syllables, often trying to imitate verbally the sounds of musical instruments; a kind of spontaneous "sound" poetry that may sound like double talk to unreceptive white ears. (Major, 1971)

3. SCAT SINGING: Jazz vocal improvisation using meaningless, often humorously suggestive syllables.

SCREAM

1. To yell at someone in a very loud and harsh manner.

2. A high shrill blow on someone.

    Situation: A child is sent to a market by his parent. The child brings back the wrong items or incorrect change. The parent scornfully castigates the child loudly and emotionally.

    Syn: To base, to blow on, jam, front off.

3. To loudtalk someone. (Andrews and Owens, 1973)

4. SCREAMIN' ON: telling someone off; i.e., getting on someone's case.
5. a gathering of close friends.

SHOWBOAT, SHOWBOATIN'

1. To show off; a slapstick comic or soft shoe; a person who has a compulsion to clown when in the presence of whites; one who elicits laughs by using stigmatized forms of Ebonics.

   Situation: A person is at a dance; there are quite a few whites and elite Negroes in attendance. This person is lower class and wants recognition. To get the recognition she desires, she talks loudly and boisterously and when the music starts she doesn't miss a dance. She does wild rubber leg dances, all over the floor until she is the center of attention.

   Syn: Jeffin'.
2. To race up and down the street in a lowered car making the lifts bounce; in sports, one who makes plays using slick moves.

SHUCKIN' AND JIVIN'

1. Talking and joking while working, especially while picking cotton and corn shucking, now work in general; akin to lolly gaggin'—joking and socializing without free time. Coinage from jazz—talking or joking while playing; musician's jargon; talking and joking while giggin.

   Situation: A person or group of people have been left unsupervised to complete a task or job. In the absence of their superior they begin to horseplay and fool around and joke on the job and not take care of business.
2. SHUCK'N JIVIN: originally southern Negro expression for clowning, lying, pretense. (Major, 1971)
3. SHUCK-FUCK: (mostly sound alike), usually only in terms of talk and action rather than the sex act. Expression is usually 'shuch' and 'jive.' See *jive*. (Abrahams, 1970)
4. SHUCKIN-AN-JIVIN: (a) Involving confrontation between blacks and the Man: language behavior designed to work on the mind and emotions of the authority figure to get him or her to feel a certain way or give up something that will be to the other's advantage. (b) When interacting with one another on a peer-group level: descriptive of the talk and gestures that are appropriate to "putting someone on" by creating a false impression, conveying false information, and the like. (c) When referring to the Black's dealings with the White Man and the power structure, the above terms (*shuckin'* and *jivin'*) are descriptive of the talk and accompanying physical movements of the Black that are appropriate to some momentary guise, posture, or facade. (Kochman, 1972)
5. SHUCK: the part of the corn plant that is no good. The meaning has extended into Black life to mean lies, deception, and inhumanity.

Shuck has come to be what Black people will not relate to. Black people can relate to corn, but they can't dig any shuckin' and jivin'. (Andrews and Owens, 1973)

SIGNIFY, SIGNIFYIN'

1. To reproach with scornful or sarcastic language; to jeer or mock; to taunt with meddlesome, irksome comments or annoying gibes. To goad or hoax two people into a fist fight by making them appear afraid of each other.

   Situation: A person wants to get someone into an encounter or conflict with someone else. They jeer and goad one into confronting the other about remarks they allegedly made about each other.

   Syn: Cappin', The Dozens, hoorahin', jonin', lug drop, cover-snatch, soundin', woofin', a toasting joke.

2. To tease with the aim of provoking anger. The signifier creates a myth about someone and tells the person that a third person started it. The signified person is aroused and seeks that person. Signifying is completely successful when the signifier convinces the chump he is working on that what he is saying is true and that it gets him angered to wrath. (Andrews and Owens, 1973)

3. To imply, goad, beg, or boast by indirect, verbal, or gestural means. A language of implication. (Abrahams, 1970)

4. *Signifying* is the term used to describe the language behavior that, as Abrahams has defined it, attempts to "imply, goad, beg, boast by indirect verbal or gestural mean."

5. Signify: same as the *Dirty Dozens;* to censure in twelve or fewer statements; see *cap on.* (Majors, 1970)

6. Signifyin', siggin(g): Language behavior that makes indirect implications of baitin' or boastin', the essence of which is making fun of another's appearance, relatives, or situation. Variations include jonin', playin' the dozens, screamin' on, soundin'. (Roberts, 1971)

SOUNDIN'

1. To test someone out by suggesting something uncomplimentary about their parents or close relatives.

   Situation: A Black teenager has recently moved into a new Black community. The teenagers who presently live in the community want to find out where his head is. In order to test him out, one of the teenagers makes a crack like, "Hey man, how is Sadie?" and the teenager may respond, "Sadie who?" and the other one cracks back with "Sadie, yo ole lady."

   Syn: Basin', blow on, cappin', dozens, high sidin', jonin', lug droppin', signifyin'.

2. The term which is today most widely used for the game of verbal insult known in the past as "playing the dozens."

Syn: signifyin', siggin', jonin', screamin'. In Chicago, sounding would describe the initial remarks that are designed to sound out the other person to see whether he will play the game. (Kochman, 1972), p. 258)

3. Soundin' (on a chick): flirting. (Major, 1971, p. 107)

SPLIB WIBBIN'

Bragging and boasting in a night club or at a party, showing off.

Situation: Often after a person wins big at the race track or some sporting event, he comes in the barber shop or his favorite club and brags about how good he can pick horses, fighters, golfers, baseball teams, etc.

STUFF PLAYIN'

A verbal trick and device; a cunning manipulative ruse used by con artist and swindlers to deceive a person for monetary gain. Stuff, i.e., worthless merchandise or nothing at all, is given in exchange for money.

Situation: A stuff player (S.P.) approaches a victim (VIC):
 S.P. "Hey boss, can you swing a deal?"
VIC. "What'ca got?"
S.P. I got sump'in I ain't got no bizness wit."
VIC "What is it?"
S.P. "You ain't gone tell if you can't use it is you?"
VIC "Naw."
S.P. shows fake jewelry).
VIC "What'cha want for em?"
S.P "All I need is some rent money."
VIC "How much is that?"
S.P. "Oh, I'm jes lakin' $50 of having it."

Syn: Cap, whup game, mackin', jeffin'.

SWEET MOUTHIN'

An enthusiastic, sometimes high-flown expression of praise. To flatter or express accolades, and adulation (usually behind the person's back) as opposed to *rappin'*, which is flattery in a person's presence.

Situation: A teacher goes to bat for a student who is in trouble with the police. As a result of the teacher's report to the court, the student is given another chance. During an open house, a school assembly or wherever she can, the student sings that teacher's praises.

Ant: Bad mouthin'.

Syn: Mackin', toastin', sing praises, rappin'.

TALKIN' PROPER

1. Flying under false colors by pretentiously using standard English.
2. The ability to mimic with mastery, the phonological, grammatical, and semantic cues of standard or formal English.

3. A hypercorrect attempt to speak standard English, characterized by excessive malaprops, paragoges, regularized verbs, and *r* sounds in the middle of words and the substitution of *r* and *a* in words ending in *a*.

Situation: A hustler who wants to impress a bank or finance company loan officer that he's reliable code switches into his best English. When asked his place of birth, for I was born in Atlanta, he says, "I were burn/d/ in Atlanter"; asked for his wife's place of employment, he said, "She wurk at alpher beter merket." In trying to further impress the banker of his reliableness, he states that he is a "ursher in the church."

Syn: Facing someone funny, puttin on airs, flying under false colors.

TALKIN' SHIT (TALKIN' TRASH)

1. Meddlesome irritating remarks that are meant to provoke a fight (See fat mouthin'); usually hearsay.
2. Sometimes refers to a heavy rap or conversation for sexual purposes.

Situation: A person working on a job has just been informed that her wages have been attached by garnishment. Some of her coworkers learn that this has occurred, and one makes a meddlesome remark, "See there, Niggah, that's what happens when you don't pay yo' bills."

Syn: Shit towin', lug' droppin', high sidin', siggin'.

3. To jive, pretend, lie. (Major, 1970, p. 113)

TALKIN' IN TONGUE

A catharsis, to become overwhelmed by the spirit of God and, while in this catatonic state, talk in unintelligible language.

Situation: A member of the Holiness or Pentecostal Black Church gets 'happy' during the sermon and goes into a stupor marked by body rigidity and continuous verbal utterances that cannot be interpreted.

TAUTIN'

To lead astray, to mislead by offering helpful advice or unsolicited information.

Situation: A person is at the race track standing in line to make a wager. He has originally intended to bet the number four horse, but someone else making conversation quotes impressive sounding statistics concerning the number eight horse. The information is so impressive the person is led to bet on the number eight horse instead of the number four horse, and he loses his money in the process.

TESTIFY, TESTIFYIN'

1. To bear witness in church. To stand and make a personal avowal of faith and belief in God.

SITUATION; In many Black churches before the services commence there is a period in which all members who desire are permitted to stand and make verbal proclamations and avowals of their belief in God and confess their foibles and sins.

2. To confess one's sins, bad deeds, life story (originally in church but now also in music, in literature and through other forms of art). (Major, 1970, p. 114)

TOAST, TOASTIN'

1. Jokes, fables, and tales which are told during social events or lunch breaks. Each person takes turns telling tall tales and poetic fables.

Situation: When Blacks are in jail, prisons, youth authority camps, and the like, they often spend their entire day telling tall tales and fables about Shine and the Titanic, Pee Wee, the pool-shootin monkey, the signifying monkey, Dolamite, etc.

2. good, fine, acceptable (adj.). (Roberts, 1971)
3. The toast is a narrative poem that is recited, often in a theatrical manner, and represents the greatest of Negro verbal talent. (Abrahams, 1970, p. 97)

TOM TOM (TOMMIN')

1. A drum for African signals.
2. A messenger, usually a trustee (Uncle Tom), who has free movement within a jail or penal institution.

Situation: A juvenile in one section of a youth authority facility wants to get a message to some of his home boys in another section. His primary and often only contact with the other section is through the trustees, who have free movement to carry his messages for him.

Syn: Grapevine, jeffin'.

3. Acting like an Uncle Tom, i.e., behaving in a self-denigrating and self-effacing manner toward a white person; ingratiating oneself with a white person. (Roberts, 1971)

WHUP, WHUPIN' GAME

Saying or doing whatever is necessary to get over, beat, cheat, or whip someone; usually a verbal deception or ruse, whupin' game can be done by acting servile, illiterate, crying, articulating carefully, or acting boisterous and flashy.

Situation: A person has no lunch money. She's hungry and she knows none of her friends have enough money individually to loan or buy her a lunch. She then goes and gets in the lunch line and, as other students pass, she states: "I'm just lacking a dime of having fifty cents for lunch." By doing this five times, she whups game for lunch.

Syn: Stuff player, cap man, J.

WOOFIN' (WOLFING)

1. Bluffing or threatening pretentiously. A verbal combat or heated exchange, usually one's scared and the other's glad of it.

Situation: Two people are verbally threatening to do each other severe bodily harm but they don't really intend to fight at all. One might say, "Nigger if you don't quit messin with me, I'm gone bust my arches in your behind." The other may reply, "Yeah, and if you do, you gone be walking around peg legged."

Syn: Basin', dozens, fat mouthin', jibbin', jonin', shuckin' and jivin', signifyin', soundin'.

2. To playfully put another person down verbally, to joke around, to talk. (Folb, 1972)

WOOF TICKET

To threaten, bluff, or extort by alluding to or intimating the use of physical violence to obtain something, usually with no intention of carrying out the threat.

Situation: The Black Student Union submits a list of ten nonnegotiable demands to the school or college administration. The administration succumbs to all ten demands without question or dispute for fear of violence on campus.

APPENDIX REFERENCES

ABRAHAMS, ROGER D. *Deep Down in the Jungle: Negro Narrative Folklore From the Streets of Philadelphia.* Chicago, Ill.: Aldine Publishing Co., 1970.

ANDREWS, MAIACHI, and PAUL T. OWENS. *Black Language.* Los Angeles: Seymour-Smith Publishing Co., 1973.

CLEAVER, ELDRIDGE. *Soul on Ice.* New York: Delta Books, 1968.

DALBY, DAVID. "The African Element in American English," in Thomas Kochman, ed., *Rappin' and Stylin' Out Communication in Urban Black America.* Chicago: University of Illinois Press, 1972.

FOLB, EDITH. *A Comparative Study of Urban Black Argot.* Washington, D.C.: Department of Health, Education and Welfare, 1972.

HASKINS, JIM, and HUGH F. BUTTS, M.D. *The Psychology of Black Language.* New York: Barnes & Nobles, 1973.

KOCHMAN, THOMAS. *Rappin' and Stylin' Out Communication in Urban Black America.* Chicago: University of Illinois Press, 1972.

MAJOR, CLARENCE. *Dictionary of Afro-American Slang.* New York: International Publishers, 1971.

ROBERTS, HERMESE E. *The Third Ear: A Black Glossary.* The Better-Speech Institute of America, 1971.

SMITH, ERNIE. "Evolution and Continuing Presence of the Oral Tradition in Black America." Doctoral Dissertation submitted to the University of California, Irvine, Fall 1974.

Webster's Seventh New Collegiate Dictionary. Springfield, Mass.: G.C. Merriam Co. Publishers, 1972.

INDEX